Schools

Educational Spaces

Schools

Sibylle Kramer

Educational Spaces

BRAUN

CONTENTS

Schools

by Sibylle Kramer

SCHOOLS – educational spaces is a collection of 60 international school buildings that were completed within the past few years. The locations of the various schools are as diverse as their building styles. This is a natural result of the various educational concepts, contents and philosophies of school systems around the world. Yet there are similarities, developments and architectural trends that define the style of schools in the 21st century and substantially affect the daily lives of students. According to a valid Swedish saying each student has three teachers – firstly the other children, secondly the teacher as such, and thirdly the educational space. In line with this

statement, architectural design has recovered its educational value in recent school construction projects. Without elaborating on the PISA study and the related discussion of educational contents, it becomes apparent at a global level that, regardless of curriculums, the design of educational spaces plays a role in the efficient use of school time. It serves not only to educate students but to help them enjoy attending school because they love their classroom or school building. Some students are happy to have a school building at all, which is not a given in all educational settings, a fact that is sometimes forgotten. In this regard, projects such as the Bamboo

School in Bangladesh are laudable because they not only educate students, but their simple construction principle also provides added educational value for local laborers, constituting a nucleus of regional development.

When looking at the list of owners and project commissioners, the school system remains largely public. While this provides planning security on the one hand, on the other hand the costs are precisely calculated, which often gets in the way of reconciling the architectural-educational concept with the construction reality. Many architectural firms, however, prove to be very creative when it comes to implementing the expanded room program with capped funds. After all, high-quality materials and a sustainable construction method have the advantage of offering durability to serve future student generations. Many school buildings from the 1970s have become in need of rehabilitation and architects need to decide whether to maintain and expand them or to construct new buildings. The appeal of both approaches is exemplified by projects such as the ISH Hamburg, a completely new construction of a school center, in which the mix of nationalities of the students is a further distinctive feature; or the expansion of the elementary school in Schulzendorf,

which not only incorporates the existing school building but also equips it with the latest state-of-the-art air conditioning technology. Almost all buildings share the fact that today their multimedia equipment is equivalent to that found in children's and adolescent's bedrooms.

Increasingly, the schools themselves provide rooms and workplaces for individual research, teamwork and work groups. Due to the advance of full-time schools they often also include a cafeteria with kitchen facilities, which constitutes an additional architectural challenge. 21st century schools not only want to convey fixed curriculum contents, but also want

to advance sports and cultural interests – with sports facilities that meet competitive standards and event halls that are the envy of some professional theaters that have almost become the norm. The frequently repeated request for color in the grey everyday school life is used to structure building sections and to create identities. Yet suitability for children should not be mistaken for childishness – after all, schools are not extended playgrounds but in the best sense mainstays of tradition and education incubators for future generations. They are treasure chests that rest on solid ground with school building projects like those presented on the following pages.

Forte, Gimenes & Marcondes
Ferraz Arquitectos

↑ | **Canopied multifunctional space**
→ | **Façade,** detail

FDE – Public School

Várzea Paulista

The building has a block with three floors and another with only the ground floor. Administrative functions, dining, kitchen and bathrooms are concentrated on the ground floor, the other floors are occupied by classrooms. The canopied hall opens to the external schoolyard. With its gates open, the school becomes an area of living for the community. The structure of the school is composed of all elements of pre-cast concrete. The structure of concrete extrapolates the limits of the building, supporting also the elements of shading. In the west façade, facing the street, concrete brick elements with openings form a large mosaic that filters the light.

PROJECT FACTS

Address: R. Cafezal/Rua Urai, S/N, Jd. América II, Várzea paulista, CEP 13220000, SP, Brazil. **Client:** Municipality of São Paulo. **Completion:** 2008. **Size:** 2,700 m². **School type:** Elementary public school. **Grades:** 1–4.

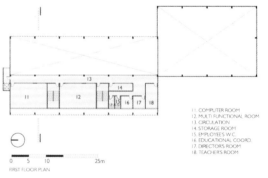

FIRST FLOOR PLAN

11. COMPUTER ROOM
12. MULTI FUNCTIONAL ROOM
13. CIRCULATION
14. STORAGE ROOM
15. EMPLOYEE'S W.C.
16. EDUCATIONAL COORD.
17. DIRECTOR'S ROOM
18. TEACHER'S ROOM

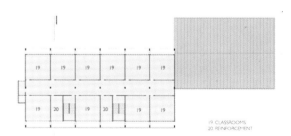

19. CLASSROOMS
20. REINFORCEMENT

↖ | Façade
← | Concrete shadows
↑ | Floor plans, section
↗ | Exterior view
→ | Front view

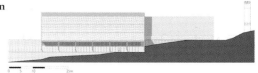

Allmann Sattler Wappner
Architekten

↑ | Exterior view
→ | Staircase

Aying Elementary School
Aying

In its scale, volume and arrangement the house-in-house concept reflects the characteristics of the rural location in the foothills of the Alps. The picture conjured by the timber
cladding is reminiscent of that of a large barn. The new school comprises 12 classrooms,
specialist rooms, administrative and teachers' rooms, a recreational area and a multi-purpose room. A special feature of the school is the way in which pupils identify with the
small school societies located in four separate houses. These structures are linked by a
central playground and thus brought together to form a single entity.

PROJECT FACTS

Address: Glonner Strasse 11, 85653 Aying, Germany. **Client:** Municipality of Aying. **Completion:** 2005. **Size:** 3,900 m².

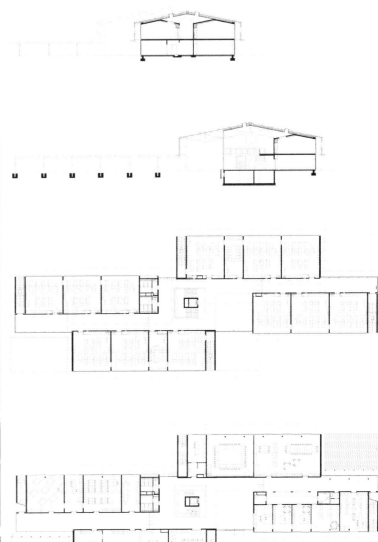

↖ | Schoolyard
← | Exterior view
↙ | Schoolyard
↑ | Hall
↗ | Sections, floor plans

↑ | Construction
→ | Exterior view

The Calhoun School

New York

The project goal aligns with the school's mission to "see the learning." This impacted how the school relates to the street and the neighborhood as well as on the activity within the building. In designing the character of the new spaces, the architect sought to heighten the fluidity of circulation between the existing and new, by use of ramps, low partitions and "commons", thereby emphasizing the communal aspects of each floor and teaching activities. The expansion added 4 stories, a mezzanine level, and filled in the building footprint of the existing five-story 1975 concrete and travertine building to add 3,000 square meters. The new addition included a green roof, the first educational institution in the City to build a green roof for educational use.

PROJECT FACTS

Address: 433 West End Avenue, New York, NY 10024, USA. **Original building:** Costas Machlouzarides (1974). **Client:** The Calhoun School. **Completion:** 2004. **Size:** 5,000 m² (existing gross area), 8,000 m² (new gross area).

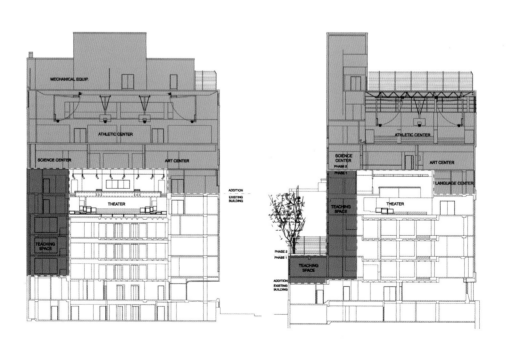

↖ | Green roof
← | Isometric model
↑ | Sections
↗ | Art classroom
→ | Theater

kramer biwer mau architekten

↑ | **Exterior view**, rendering
→ | **Auditorium**, rendering
↘ | **Site plan**

ISH International School

Hamburg

The architects of the new International School at Hemmingstedter Weg have designed a building which serves the objective to offer a quiet ambiance for the education of pupils of different nations and cultures. It is the architects' idea to follow the desire of pupils and parents to have an unpretentious architecture which serves as a temporary anchorage far-off from one's native country. An international school sports programme requires facilities of the highest level in order to host international school sporting events. The facilities will be state of the art and will include a fully equipped double size gymnasium, outdoor basketball courts, an outdoor sports field and a climbing wall. In order to enhance the school's strong traditions in the Performing Arts, at the heart of the new International School Hamburg will be a Performing Arts Center.

PROJECT FACTS

Address: Hemmingstedter Weg 130, 22607 Hamburg, Germany. **Client:** International School Hamburg e.V. **Completion:** 2009 (ongoing). **Size:** 17,000 m². **School type:** all-day school with kindergarden and double gym.

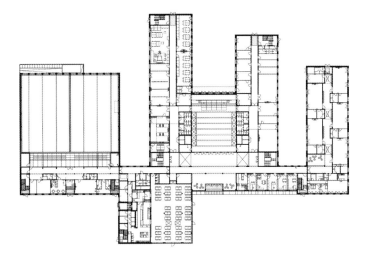

↑ | **Floor plan**
↗ | **Façade**, detail
→ | **Reading garden**
↘ | **Interior view**
↓ | **Exterior view**

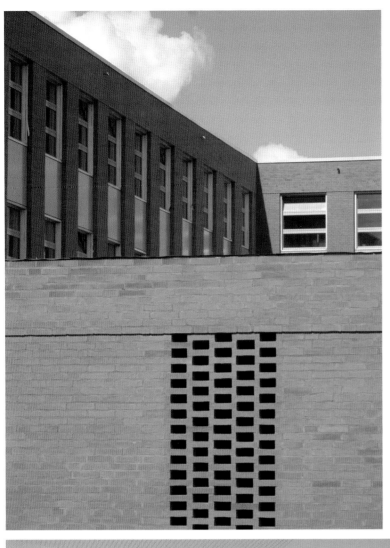

↑ | **Staircase**
→ | **Exterior**, night view

Ørestad College

Copenhagen

Ørestad College is the first college in Denmark based on the new visions of content, subject matter, organisation and learning systems in the reform of the educational system of the Danish "high-school" (gymnasium) for students of the age of 16–19. Communication, interaction and synergy has been key issues. The project displays a visionary interpretation of openness and flexibility regarding team sizes, varying from the individual over groups to classes and assemblies, and reflects international tendencies aiming at achieving a more dynamic and life-like studying environment and introducing IT as a main tool. The intention is also to enforce the students' abilities to care for own learning, both through teamwork and individual assignments.

PROJECT FACTS

Address: Ørestad Gymnasium, Ørestad Boulevard 75, 2300 Copenhagen, Denmark. **Client:** Municipality of Copenhagen & Danish University and Property Agency under the Ministry of Science, Technology and Innovation. **Completion:** 2007. **Size:** 12,000 m².

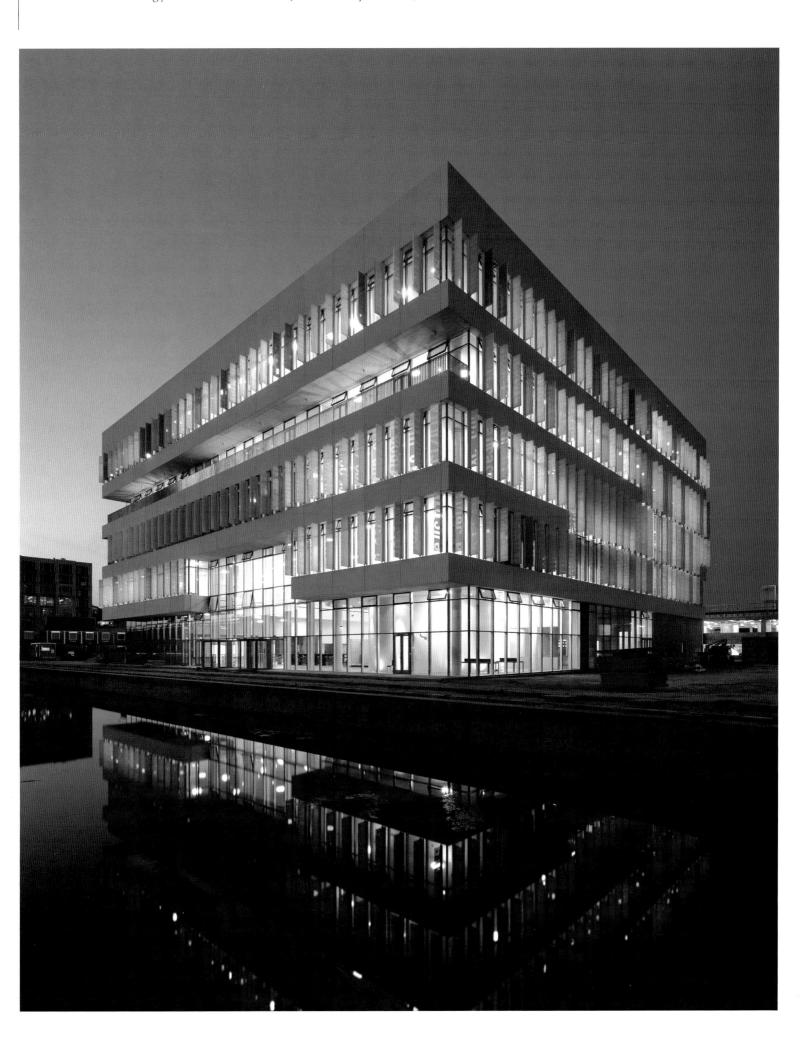

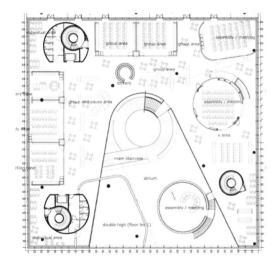

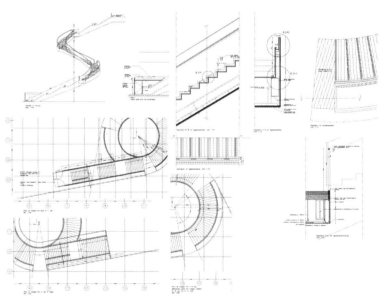

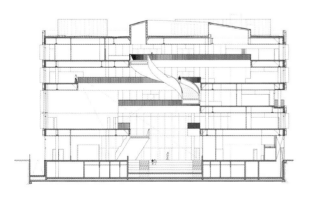

↖ | **Floor plan**, staircase spiral
↑ | **Interior view**
← | **Section**
→ | **Furniture**

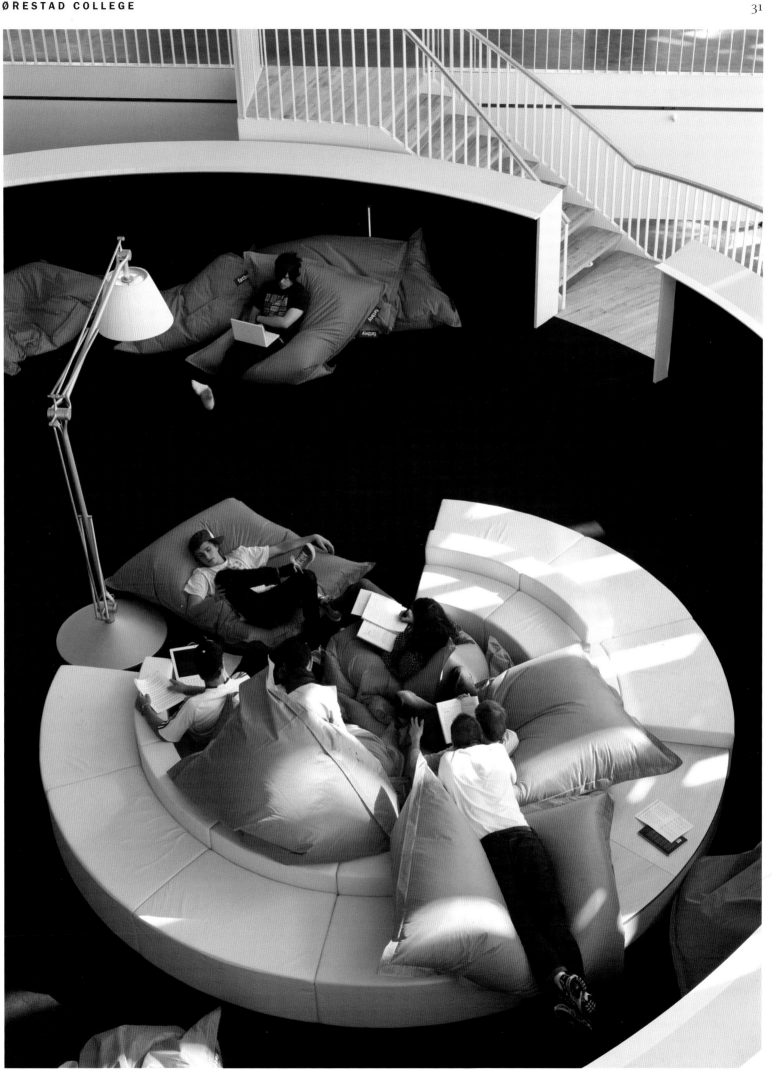

Aeschlimann Prêtre Hasler
Architekten

↑ | **External view**
→ | **Façade corner,** detail

Lower Grade School Building
Burgdorf

The new building forms a coherent group with the existing school and the gym. The place-
ment creates spatial relations, that strengthen the identity of the place and clearly show
the width of the Lindefeld. The two covered areas connect the building with the outside
and create something like a lobby. Next to the lobby we find an atrium and a gallery bring-
ing light to the inner corridors. The spatial diversity, with its range of different room se-
quences represents a stimulating dynamic "school world", connected in many ways with
its environment. The school integrates the depth of the Lindefeld and vice versa.

PROJECT FACTS

Address: Zähringerstrasse 25, 3400 Burgdorf, Switzerland. **Client:** Municipality of Burgdorf.
Other creatives involved: Mebatech AG. **Completion:** 2005.

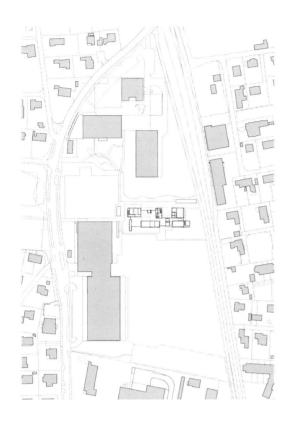

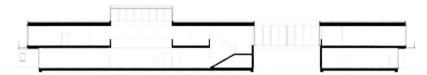

↖ | Site plan, section
↓ | External view
→ | Internal view
↘ | Insight

↑ | Entrance to schoolyard
→ | Creative areas

Lorentzschool
Leiden

This primary school for 900 pupils contains not only a multimedia library but also a play-room with after-school group and a gymnasium. In the center of the school, easily acces-sible from all directions is the heart of the school: the Auditorium. This multifunctional space can be transformed into a ballroom with foyer, gallery and theater for monthly per-formances. Many ways can be used to approach the school, but most of them meet again in the center. Sliding doors to the classrooms and huge windows bring light to the inner corridors and create an open learning atmosphere.

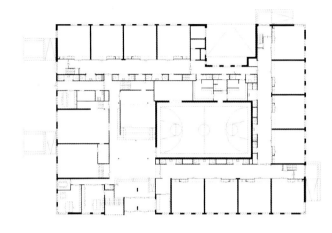

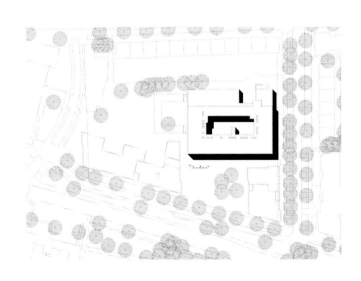

↖↖ | **Multifunctional use of stairs**
← | **Classroom** with sliding door
↗ | **Floor plan, site plan**
↑ | **Schoolyard**
← | **View to library / media**

↑ | **General view**
→ | **Façade**, detail

Expansion Catholic School
Cologne

By 2009, the city of Cologne redesigned all 161 urban elementary schools for an all-day use. Including the Catholic primary school in the south of Cologne, where on the court-yard side, a new wing was necessary to ensure the required space for additional group rooms, a kitchen and a dining area. The cost for the 460 square meters extension amount-ed to a total of 2.6 million euros. The sculptural form of the new building derives from two goals: keeping as much schoolyard surface as possible and observing the distance to the neighboring buildings. The small glass tiles in different green colors cover the entire visible surface of the building. The combination of glass tiles with a thermal insulation composite façade is being used for the first time.

PROJECT FACTS

Address: Mainzer Strasse 30–34, 50678 Cologne, Germany. **Client:** Municipality of Cologne. **Completion:** 2007. **Size:** 1,200 m². **School type:** all-day school. **Grades:** 1–4.

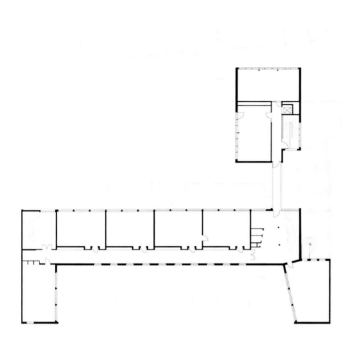

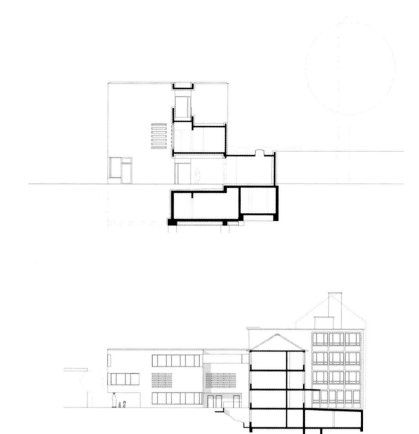

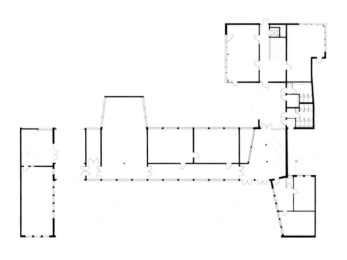

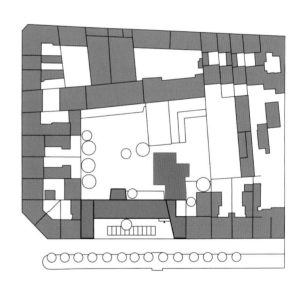

↑ | **Sections and site plan**
← | **Floor plans**
↗ | **Front view**
→ | **Mosaic,** detail

Diezinger & Kramer

↑ | **View from schoolyard**
→ | **Interior view**

Public Middle School
Eching

The school located on the northwest outskirts of the town, between track and housing development and on the border to the open landscape desires the definition of a significant location. Because of the special location and the quite big distance to the city center the school is designed as a self-sufficient urban place. The new kronstruction, consisting of a three floor school building and gym was created for approximately 1,000 pupils. The structure of the building seems to be closed to the exterior but is discontinued on distinctive points:In the north it is open to the landscape through the school yard, in the south the access is deepened in the ground level and shows up interesting views. And in the east the triple gym is one level lower and upstream to get a comfortable benchmark. Interior the central recreation area has different functions: sheltering, event, meeting point and allocation.

PROJECT FACTS
Address: Untere Hauptstrasse 3, 85386 Eching, Germany. **Client:** Municipality of Freising.
Completion: 2006. **Size:** 12,629 m².

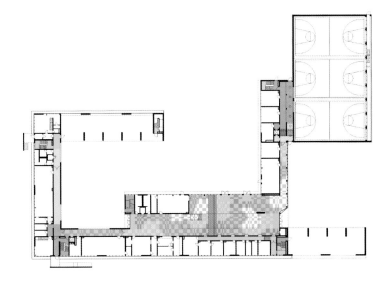

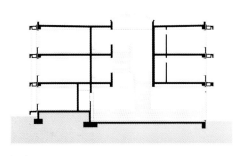

↖ | Façade
↙ | Classroom
← | Floor plan, section
↓ | Bird's eye view

$$x^2 - 4x - 1 = 0$$

$$\vdots - \mathbb{T}.$$

$$\vdots = 2 \pm \sqrt{4 + 1}$$

$$= 4{,}24$$

Block Period

pbr Planungsbüro Rohling AG

↑ | **Exterior view**
→ | **Interior view**

Strittmatter-Gymnasium

Gransee

The new building of the Strittmatter-Gymansium in Gransee is designed as a two-floor comb-like structure opening up towards the schoolyard. By utilizing the slightly offset premises towards the Oranienburg street, a garden floor was created and primarily used for extracurricular activities. The two-storied looy contains the cafeteria, teacher's lounge, multi-purpose room, and janitor's room. The "comb teeth" structures south of the hall contain the general classrooms of the lower secondary level, north of this are the classes for the senior secondary level, while the specialized classrooms are located in the section facing the Oranienburg street. Light and friendly colors accentuate the school building.

Address: Oranienburger Strasse 30a, 16775 Gransee, Germany. **Client:** Landkreis Oberhavel. **Other creatives involved:** Anton Anneser, Heinrich Eustrup, Hartmut Rohling, Ursula Werner. **Completion:** 2005. **Size:** 5,467 m². **Grades:** 7–13.

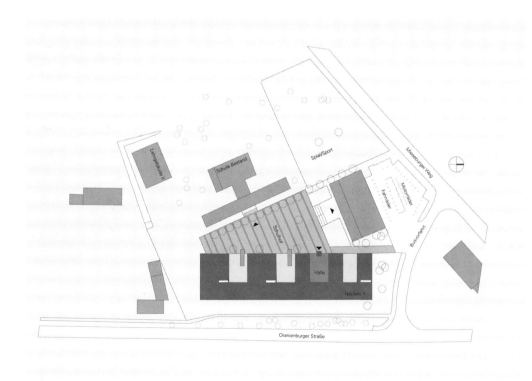

← | Site plan
↑ | Hall
→ | Entrance

↑ | **Exterior view**
→ | **Interior view**, lobby

New Tech High
Coppell

An existing school was transformed from a typical building to a remarkable, more transparent environment intentionally linked to the world beyond its walls. The building fosters connections between spaces while the curriculum further adheres to this philosophy with project-based learning. Meeting spaces can literally be created anywhere in the floor plan which, at any given time, is saturated with learners collaborating on their own projects. Realizing our new digital world has a marked impact on the way students learn, the district and architects created an environment that provides opportunities for students to readily integrate available technology into all aspects of their learning experience.

PROJECT FACTS

Address 113 Samuel Boulevard, Coppell, TX 75019, USA. **Client:** Coppell ISD. **Completion:** 2008.
Size: 5,800 m².

↖ | **Overall view**
←← | **Night view,** entrance
↑ | **Students between classes**
← | **View to classroom**

Daniele Marques
Marques AG

↑ | **View from northwest**
→ | **Schoolyard**

School Building Hinter Gärten
Riehen

The quarter is dominated by single and multiple family homes with various heights. The project reacts to this setting with a composition of high and low individual structures, which are assimilated for various stages and functions and connected via covered outdoor spaces. The greenery of the complex highlights the impression of an open continuous room and connects the new school to the neighborhood gardens. The buildings are clearly laid out and the various utilization areas are divided into convenient spatial units. In conjunction with the interior color concept, this lay-out supports the identification of the rooms and aids the orientation inside the building.

PROJECT FACTS **Address:** Steingrubenweg 30, 4125 Riehen, Switzerland. **Client:** Municipality of Basel. **Completion:** 2006. **Size:** 4,629 m². **Type:** primary school. **Number of grades:** 8.

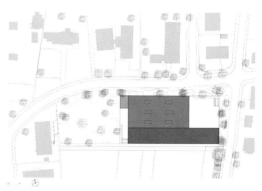

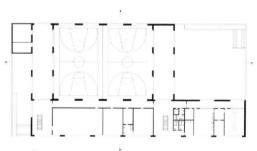

↑ | **Gym, floor plan, section**
← | **Hall**, detail
↗ | **Furniture**
→ | **Entrance**

no w here architekten and
SeiboldBloss

↑ | **Children's rehearsal room**
→ | **Exterior view**

Domsingschule

Stuttgart

The architects have responded to the complex design demands of a choral school with
an equally complex and well-considered concept. In terms of how it relates to its urban
context, the new building has been successfully integrated into its heterogeneous environment with a sensitive understanding of scale and a use of materials that reflects and
reinterprets local building practice. The folded configuration adopted for the outer skin
of the building is consistently mirrored in the treatment of the interior. The brick used
for the outer skin is replaced by bamboo on the inside – a timber that responds well to in-
door temperature and humidity. In order to reduce sound reverberation times in the practice rooms to the required minimum, a complex system of acoustic panels with varying
sound-absorbing and sound-reflecting characteristics was installed. The lighting design
of the building takes both rehearsal needs and concert situations into account.

PROJECT FACTS
Address: Landhausstrasse 29, 70191 Stuttgart, Germany. **Client:** Catholic congregation Stuttgart.
Completion: 2006/07. **Size:** 2,000 m². **School type:** music school. **Classes:** from the age of 6.

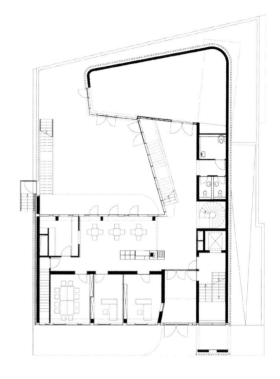

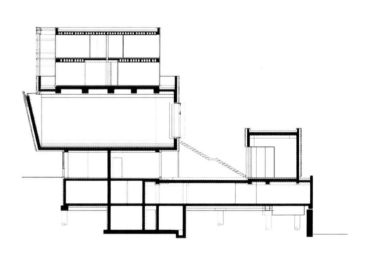

↖ | **Corner,** exterior view

← | **Stairase**

↑ | **Floor plan, section**

↗ | **Main façade**

→ | **Main rehearsal room,** detail

↑ | **Playground**
→ | **Exterior view**

Adharshila Vatika

New Delhi

The design required five to six classrooms with a capacity for 30 children. The client wanted the character of a kindergarden school with the use of pastel shades. The two storied building was placed at the middle of the site, so all rooms have natural ventilation. The plan was kept as simple as possible and only had one corridor connecting all the spaces. The hexagonal shape of the building encloses an open courtyard, that acts as a secured playground. The building elevation derives from basic forms of circle, triangle and square and is intended to look modern instead of an old castle or fairy tale exterior. The selection of colors used outside and inside the building avoided dark or bright colors like red, green or orange.

PROJECT FACTS
Address: Opposite A-56, part 1, Gujrawala Tow, Gt. Karnal Road, New Delhi, 110009 India.
Client: Mr. Vijay Goel. **Completion:** 2008. **Size:** 700 m².

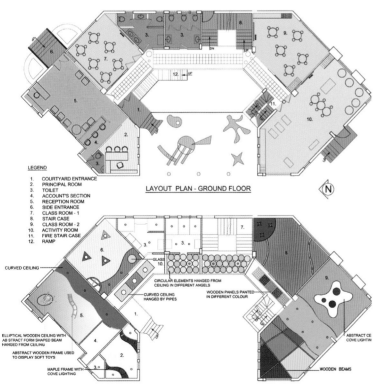

LEGEND

1. COURTYARD ENTRANCE
2. PRINCIPAL ROOM
3. TOILET
4. ACCOUNT'S SECTION
5. RECEPTION ROOM
6. SIDE ENTRANCE
7. CLASS ROOM - 1
8. STAIR CASE
9. CLASS ROOM - 2
10. ACTIVITY ROOM
11. FIRE STAIR CASE
12. RAMP

LAYOUT PLAN - GROUND FLOOR

CURVED CEILING

CURVED CEILING
HANGED BY PIPES

CIRCULAR ELEMENTS HANGED FROM
CEILING IN DIFFERENT ANGLES

WOODEN PANELS PANTED
IN DIFFERENT COLOUR

ELLIPTICAL WOODEN CEILING WITH
ABSTRACT FORM SHAPED BEAM
HANGED FROM CEILING

ABSTRACT WOODEN FRAME USED
TO DISPLAY SOFT TOYS

MAPLE FRAME WITH
COVE LIGHTING

ABSTRACT CE
COVE LIGHTIN

WOODEN BEAMS

CEILING PLAN - GROUND FLOOR

↑ | Hall
← | Floor plans
↗ | Interior view
→ | Entrance

deffner voitländer
architekten bda

↑ | **Entrance yard**
→ | **Night view**

Primary School Augustenfeld
Dachau

The two-floor, almost square structure of the school is reduced to a strictly orthogonal outer shape, divided by polygonal inserted inner courtyards. The shifting walls offer several surfaces reflecting the light at various angles, while at the same time defining and staging the shared space of the auditorium and courtyards. The color concept supports the spatial concept – mud grey on the outside as the surrounding bog landscape. In contrast to this, the interior bursts in shades of red–orange. The monochrome concept of the façades is achieved by using the same color on all materials. All other rooms are kept neutral and uncolored. The wide hallways support various educational approaches.

PROJECT FACTS

Address: Geschwister-Scholl-Strasse 4, 85221 Dachau, Germany. Client: Municipality of Dachau. Completion: 2006. Size: 3,880 m². Grades: 1–4.

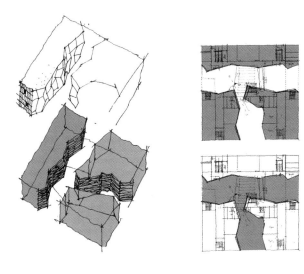

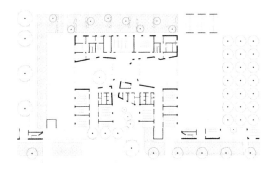

↖ | Drawings, floor plan
← | Entrance to the classroom yard
↙ | Red stair tower
←← | Space between classrooms
↓ | Exterior view

Free Period

↑ | **Exterior view**
→ | **Façade**, detail

Primary School and Library
Saint-Gingolph

Incorporating the building into the surrounding landscape was the key factor in choosing the materials in the project planning stage. A building in which the roof is as visible as the side façades requires a common material for the entire outer skin. For this purpose, considering the intensive use of the building, exposed concrete was chosen. This material allows the construction of a building with an excellent energy balance.

PROJECT FACTS
Address: Chemin des Rasses, 1898 Saint-Gingolph, Switzerland. **Client:** Municipality of Saint-Gingolph. **Completion:** 2008.

← | Hall
↙ | Façade
↓ | Floor plan, section, elevation
→ | Classroom
↘ | View on the roof

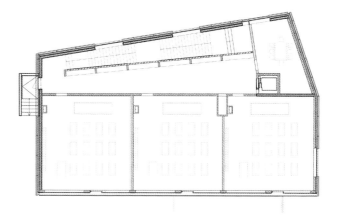

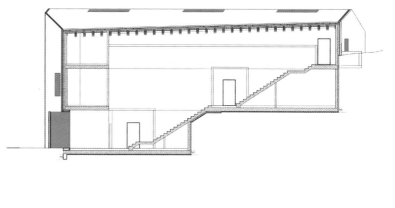

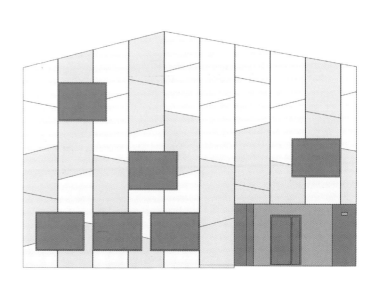

Maryann Thompson
Architects with Ingrid Strong

↑ | **Window louvers modulate sunlight**
→ | **Exterior view with roofs**

The Children's School
Stamford

The design of this school was conceived as a "one-room schoolhouse". The roof planes
subtly tilt against one another to allow light into the learning spaces that are defined without the use of walls. The scheme creates a fragmented reading of the building, appropriat-
ing the scale of the building to that of a child. Designed to achieve LEED certification, this
project treads lightly on earth while heightening the student's sense of relationship to the
site. The passive solar design with cross ventilation lowers the overall heating and cooling
demands. The building opens to the South for maximum solar gain with window louvers
modulating the summer sun on the South and West elevations. Covered outdoor spaces
form an extension of the interior learning spaces.

PROJECT FACTS Address: 118 Scofieldtown Road, Stamford, CT 06903, USA. **Completion:** 2007. **Size:** 1,300 m². **School type:** private / early education.

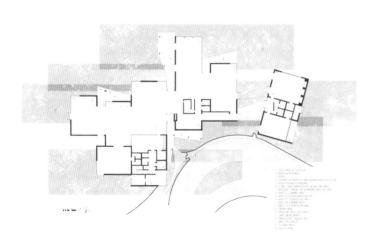

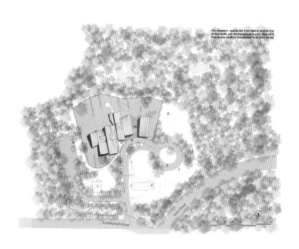

↖↖ | Science and art room
←← | Exterior view
↑↑ | Interior view, library
↑← | Floor plans and sections

Georg Scheel Wetzel
Architects

↑ | **Exterior view**
→ | **Hall**

Foundation Institute for the Blind

Regensburg

The Blind Institute Regensburg and boarding school is a school for children and young people with blindness or visual impairments and other disabilities. Here they learn to act independently, according to their individual skills and prepare for adult life. Even the smallest detail helps the students to learn without the classic blind practice guidelines: scenes with different lighting, room acoustics, contrast and level differences and special material surfaces. In close coordination with the Institute of the Blind Foundation, the architects developed and implemented a clever concept.

PROJECT FACTS

Address: An der Brunnenstube 31, 93051 Regensburg, Germany. **Client:** Foundation Institute for the Blind Würzburg, Germany. **Completion:** 2005. **Size:** 12,000 m².

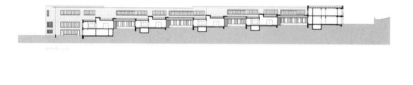

↑↑ | Overall view
↖ | Sections
↗ | Gym
↑ | Floor plan
→ | Hall

Jean-Patrice Calori
CAB architectes

↑ | View from the road
→ | View from the schoolyard

Lycée Jules Ferry
Cannes

With this construction, three existing buildings merge into an new ensemble: the boarding school, the studios and administrative offices. This new ensemble also fits well in the urban context. The conversion took place in three phases: the restructuring of the old boarding school, the distribution of the studios into two new buildings and the construction of a new administration building. Level differences have been equalized by creating new stairs in the schoolyard. Low walls, offering outdoor seatings, run along the path, dividing the yard into rest areas and sports areas.

Address: Boulevard de la république 82, 06402, Cannes France. Client: Region PACA.
Completion: 2003. Size: 8,400 m². Number of grades: 4.

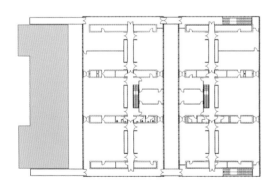

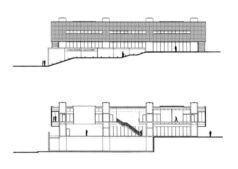

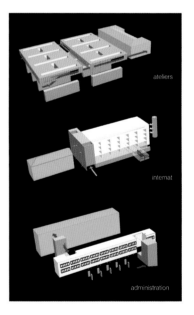

ateliers

internat

administration

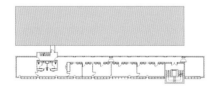

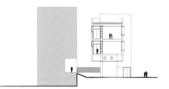

↖ | Exterior view
↑ | Axonometry
← | Floor plans, sections
→ | Interior view

CPG Consultants Pte. Ltd.

↑ | **Exterior view**
↗ | **Learning environment**
→ | **Foyer**

GEMS World Academy
Dubai

Designed by Singaporean based architects CPG, GEMS World Academy will offer an un-paralleled learning environment and opportunities for students and their families. From Kindergarten level to Grade-12, this international school accommodates 2,440 pupils on a 4.2 hectare site. The concept of sharing and exchanging between clusters of learning hubs gives birth to a communal learning environment which sets a new paradigm to reflect the latest thinking in education and a new benchmark for schools of the future. The building design captures the poetic undulations of the sand dunes through its meandering form and flowing roof, softening the otherwise harsh environment.

PROJECT FACTS

Address: Gems World Academy, PO Box 126260 Al Barsha South, Dubai, United Arab Emirates. **Client:** GEMS Education. **Completion:** 2010. **Size:** 35,000 m². **School type:** international school. **Grades:** from kindergarden to grade 12.

← | Section, floor plan
↓ | Frontage with blue backdrop
→ | Façade, night view
↘ | Hub of science

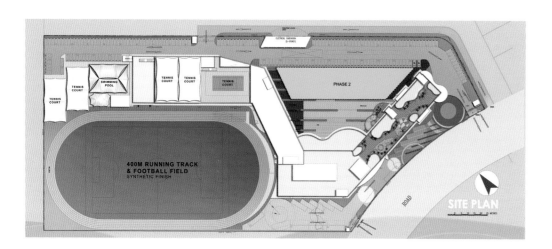

Behnisch,
Behnisch & Partner
now Behnisch Architekten

↑→| External view

Wilhelm-Busch-Schule
Illertissen

The new school for children with special learning needs is situated at the edge of the town of Illertissen, at the boundary between the town and the open landscape. Here, children and young people requiring special pedagogic attention will spend the first years of school life, and here they will learn to manage their daily affairs and to live together in a community. The compact two-storey complex is characterised by three houses accommodating the various functions. A central hall with a partly glazed roof is the communicative heart of the complex. This hall, which is oriented towards the town, is intended as both a general meeting place and as a setting for all kinds of school events.

PROJECT FACTS
Address: Jedesheimer Kirchenweg 2, 89257 Illertissen, Germany. **Client:** Municipality of Neu-Ulm.
Completion: 2004. **Size:** 1,540 m². **School type:** school for children with special learning needs.

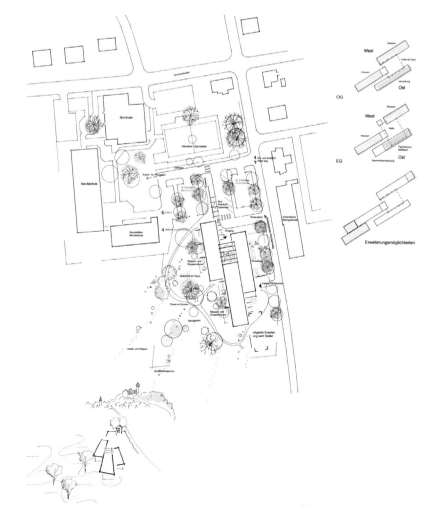

↑ | Corridor
← | Site plan
↗ | Hall
→ | Entrance

↑ | **Night view**
→ | **Façade,** detail

Extension School Stefanacci
San Piero a Sieve

The extension of the primary and secondary school in San Piero a Sieve is very close to the city of Florence. It is composed according to the character and the materials of the Tuscan countryside projected in a contemporary horizon. The building consists of two rectangular volumes covered with white plaster, which are orientated differently. The main volume is defined by a big solid wall containing a small auditorium and the main corridor illuminated from the ceiling. The smaller volume, illuminated by windows with a variety of dimensions, is organized on two levels containing offices, laboratories and a small library.

PROJECT FACTS

Address: Via trifilò 2, 50037 San Piero a Sieve (Fi), Italy. **Client:** Municipality of San Piero a Sieve. **Completion:** 2009. **Size:** 690 m².

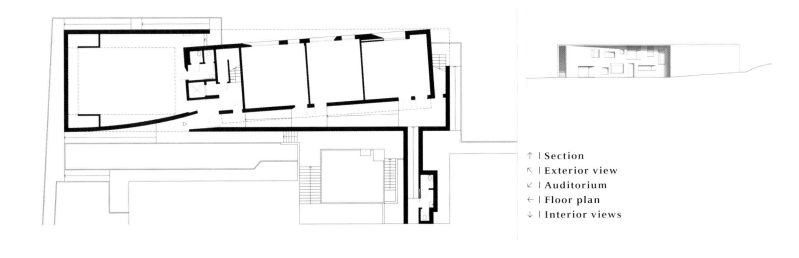

↑ | Section
↖ | Exterior view
↙ | Auditorium
← | Floor plan
↓ | Interior views

mattes · sekiguchi partner
architekten bda

↑ | General view
→ | Canopied schoolyard

Selma-Rosenfeld-Realschule

Eppingen

The angular, in part elevated, extension of the existing u-shaped structure provides the school with a partially roofed playground and the urban development style of a campus. In addition to the full-time school section, the extension includes extra classrooms and specialized rooms. Based on the existing structure of 2001, the façade was covered with an insulated, rear ventilated construction of façade plates. Room-high aluminum façade elements were implemented in the classrooms and specialized rooms. Inside, the materials are limited to smoothly finished exposed concrete ceilings, exposed concrete walls with a structured finish, acoustic wall elements, and drywall acoustic friezes in the class rooms.

PROJECT FACTS
Address: Berliner Ring 22, 75031 Eppingen, Germany. **Client:** Municipality of Eppingen.
Completion: 2007. **Size:** 1,404 m². **Type of school:** secondary school. **Classes:** 5–10.

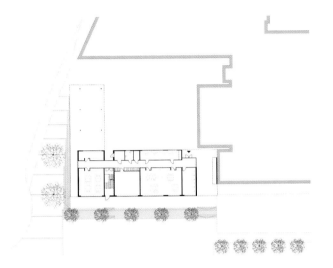

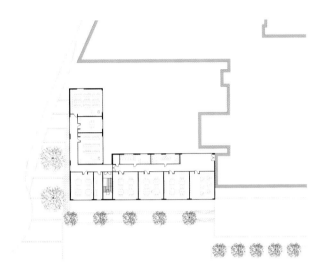

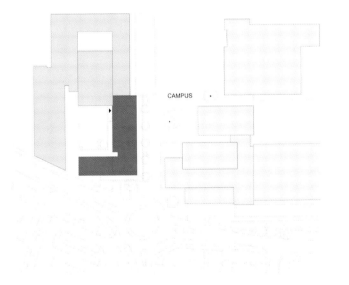

CAMPUS

↖↖ | Classroom
←← | Hall
↑ | Floor plans
↖ | Siteplan
↗ | Section

↑ | **Exterior view**
→ | **Interior view**, library

Cantonal School Rychenberg
Winterthur

Classified as a historical monument today, the cantonal school Im Lee was built from 1926–28 by the brothers Pfister in the monumental style of the times. In its direct vicinity, the cantonal school Rychenberg, which is also listed, was erected between 1960 and 1963 by Erik Lanter in the traditional Corbusian style. To the west of this area, architects Stutz und Bolt created an addition with special rooms and canteen in 1990. The challenge was to add an adequate building to this ensemble of charismatic buildings. The room plan – consisting of a triple gymnasium with a weights and gymnastics room, a media library for 150 users, a music wing with two lecture rooms and a hall for musical events, 11 class-rooms and underground parking space for 500 bicycles – was placed on a narrow, still un-exploited strip of land between the school premises and the sports field. The whole urban composition, spanning several decades, was enriched by a new, unique voice embedded harmoniously into the existing context.

Address: Rychenbergstrasse 110, Winterthur, Switzerland. **Client:** Kantonales Hochbauamt Zürich. **Completion:** 2008. **Size:** 8,720 m².

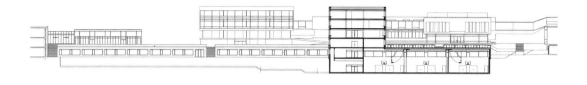

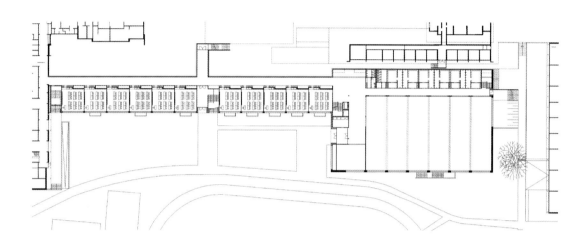

↑ | Floor plan
↓ | Site plan
← | Gym
↗ | Overall view
→ | Niche with pupils

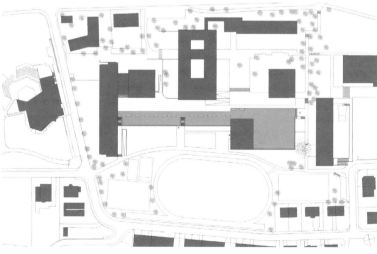

Break

Gordon Murray + Alan Dunlop
Architects

↑ | **Bird's eye view**
→ | **Interior view**

Hazelwood School

Glasgow

Hazelwood school is a facility for up to 60 students with multiple disabilities. The building curves around the existing trees of the site. Inside, the curved form of the building reduces the visual scale of the main circulation spaces and helps remove the institutional feel. Navigation and orientation through the building and independence for the children were key concerns. A tactile wall aids orientation and mobility and doubles as a storage for the large pieces of equipment that are a daily requirements for most students. The design team developed a palette of highly textured natural materials that stimulate the children's touch and smell. Naturally weathering timber boarding, reclaimed slate tiles and zinc were chosen for variety and contrast.

PROJECT FACTS
Address: 50 Dumbreck Court, Glasgow G41 5DQ, UK. **Client:** Glasgow City Council. **Completion:** 2009. **Size:** 2,666 m². **Grades:** from nursery up to 19 years of age.

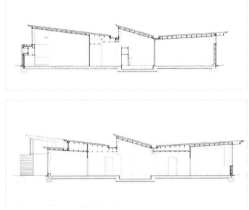

← | Schoolyard
↙ | Outside view
↖ | Sensuary wall
↗ | Sections
↓ | Site plan

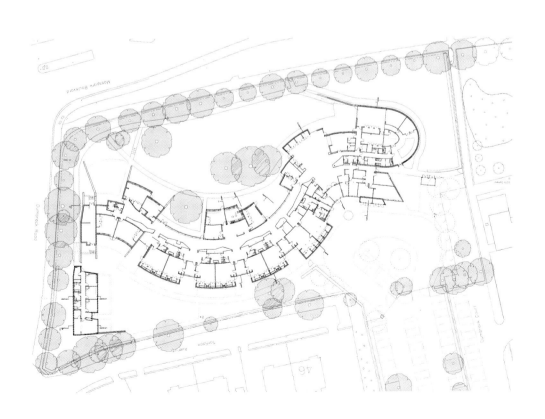

rheinpark_Architekten

↑ | **Exterior view**
→ | **Bird's eye view**

Secondary and Elementary School
Holzkirchen

The building site was discoverd to be a lowered cow paddock. To enable a connection to the neighboring meadows, a vegetated landscape plate with a size of 180 x 70 meters was placed into the four meters deep syncline. Four yards, cut into the plate illuminate the classrooms, the gymnasium and the lower entrance area. The class houses with typical bavarian dark wood paneling are situated on the grass roof. By this, a school with two ground floors arises. As picture puzzle between nature and artificiality the project regenerates the local landscape of the district of Miesbach. Energetically the meadow roof with the concrete core serves as heating and cooling.

Address: Probst-Sigl-Strasse 5–7, 83607 Holzkirchen, Germany. **Client:** Municipality of Miesbach, Markt Holzkirchen. **Completion:** 2005. **Size:** 12,719 m².

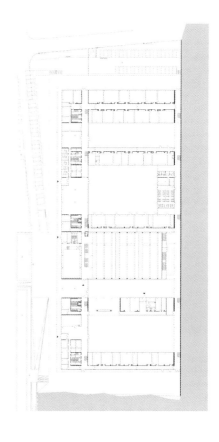

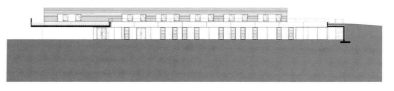

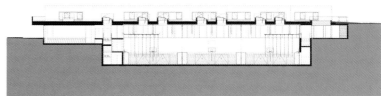

↖ | **Staircase**, detail
← | **Site plan**
↑ | **Floor plan, sections**
↗ | **External view**
→ | **View from schoolyard**

↑ | **Overall view**
→ | **Bamboo structure**

Bamboo School
Nha Trang City

A French NGO L'École Sauvage would like to build a primary school for street children in a very poor suburb of Nha Trang City, a coastal city in the center of Vietnam. Very quickly, the idea to use bamboo as a main construction material came true. In effect in Vietnam this plant is very common and cheap. L'École Sauvage was associated with Ministry of Education of Vietnam to build a six classrooms school. Some planted patios allow natural ventilation and also natural light. The construction took place in only six months, due to the use of prefabricated elements and repeat modules. In this project there was no need for high technology or technique. The simple school building point out an alternative to modern architecture made from concrete and glass.

PROJECT FACTS

Address: Luong Son Village, Nha Trang City, Vietnam. **Client:** L'École Sauvage (French NGO), The Ministery of Education of Vietnam. **Completion:** 2005. **Size:** 550 m². **Grades:** Public elementary school, later some secondary classes.

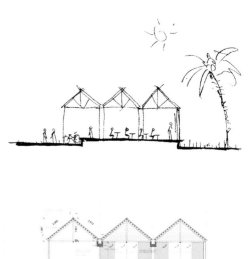

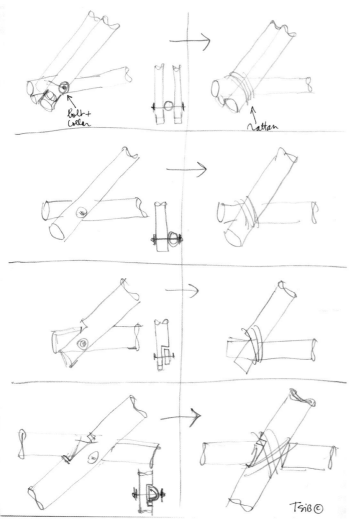

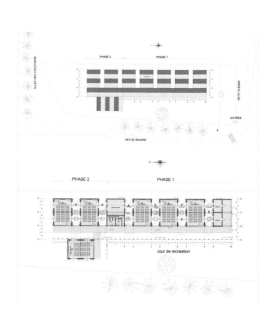

↑ | Sections, floor plan
⤴ | Bamboo structures
→ | Classrooms

HERLE + HERRLE Architekten
BDA

↑ | **Bridge crossing schoolyard**
→ | **Hall**

Secondary School
Kösching

The new building was constructed for a six-year secondary school, including a double gymnasium and outdoor exercise facilities. Located at the edge of Kösching, the school building consists of three building sections that constitute a rectangular structure fitted around a green inner courtyard. Together with the double gymnasium, this constitutes the boundaries of the schoolyard. The appearance is dominated by the shifting, reddish surface structure of the corten steel façade plates.

PROJECT FACTS

Address: Ingolstädter Strasse 111, 85092 Kösching, Germany. **Client:** Municipality of Eichstätt.
Other creatives involved: Doris Grabner (landscape architecture), Peter Baron (façade design).
Completion: 2006. **Size:** 8,115 m².

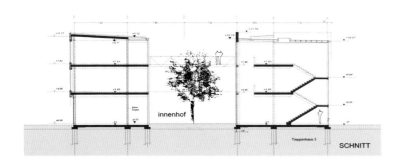

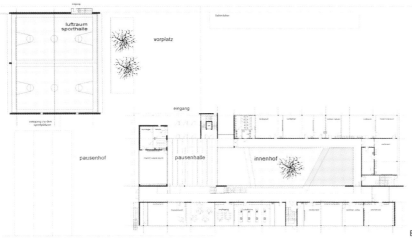

↖ | **Bridge**, detail
↑ | **Siteplan**
← | **Section**, floor
→ | **Façade**, corten

↑ | **Exterior view**
→ | **Staircase**

Daltonschool Columbus

Heerhugowaard

The Multifunctional center Daltonschool Columbus is situated between trees in a large park. The school consists of 14 class-rooms, a day care center and a gymnasium. By placing the auditorium and the playroom in the central space of the building, they become 'the heart' of the organisation. The 'heart' connects three different levels and provides visual and spatial contact between the class-rooms, the day care center and the gymnasium. To moderate daylight in the school, PV cells have been applied in the glass, thus creating an interesting interplay between light and shadow.

PROJECT FACTS

Address: Weegbree 2, Heerhugowaard, The Netherlands. **Client:** Municipality of Heerhugowaard.
Other creatives involved: Dorte Kristensen and Lissette Plouvier. **Completion:** 2007. **Size:** 3,020 m².

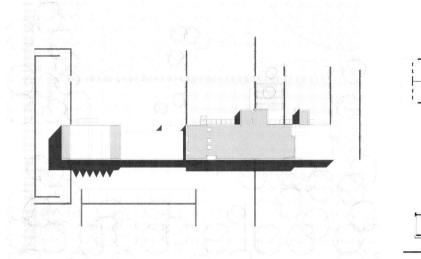

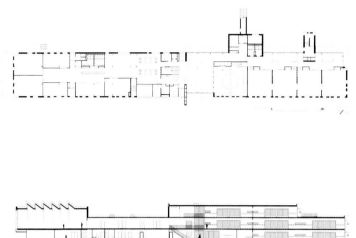

↖ | Site plan, sections
←↙| Interior views
↓ | Overall view

Ramón Pico Valimana
Javier López Rivera

↑ | **Entrance**
→ | **View from the street**

Reyes Católicos Primary School
Cádiz

"..only blind, good and dumb children of the school have not known those raging trembling hours, full of wind and salts, of the salt marshes white, enough to soak the entire life of an infinite blue light..." (Rafael Alberti). Probably one of the greatest challenges faced by architects is the construction of a school. The experience acquired in their own biography, the lacks and joys of their own childhood, are going to constantly affect the decisions of the project and the work. In this case, with Alberti's words as a background, our obsession focused on the search for those singular spaces, "magic" spaces that fit the concept of the school as a place to learn, to be educated and to have fun.

PROJECT FACTS
Address: Av. Ana de Viya 36, corner with calle Fernandez Ballesteros, Cádiz, Spain. **Client:** Consejeria de Educcion, Junta de Andalucia. **Completion:** 2005. **Size:** 3,025 m².

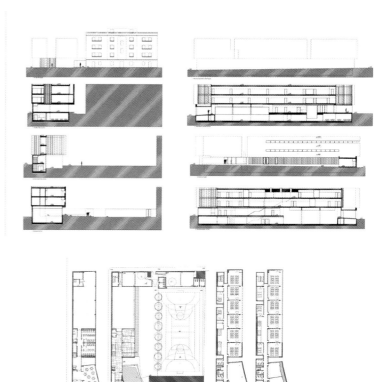

← | Staircase
↑ | Sections, floor plan
↙ | School yard
→ | Façade
↗ | Gym
↘ | Interior view

Studio Andreas Heller GmbH

↑ | **Exterior view**
→ | **Façade,** detail

Forum Johanneum

Hamburg

The extension of one of Germany's most renown high schools stems from a project in-
volving in equal parts a patron, the Hamburg Department of Culture, and the designated
architects of the Studio Andreas Heller. The new construction consists of an ensemble
that restructured the previous use of the Johanneum. The move of the fine arts classes,
including art, music and theater, some of which are offered across all grade levels, from
the old to the new building allowed the positioning of the individual grade levels in the
vicinity of the historical Fritz Schumacher building of 1914. In addition, the new building
was complemented by a gymnasium with a small visitor's stand and a cafeteria/canteen.

PROJECT FACTS

Address: Maria-Louisen-Strasse 114, 22301 Hamburg, Germany. **Client:** Forum Johanneum GmbH. **Other creatives involved:** Sona Kazemi. **Completion:** 2007. **Size:** 2,574 m². **School type:** humanistic grammar school. **Grades:** 5–12.

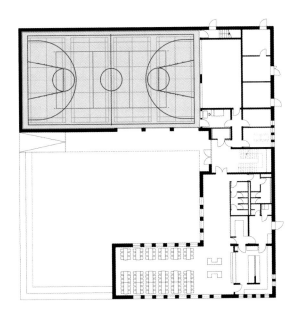

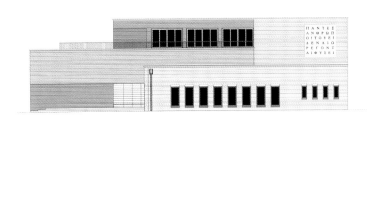

← | Schoolyard
↙ | Auditorium
↑ | Floor plan, sections
↓ | Exterior view

↑ | **Night view**
→ | **Façade**, detail

Jackson Community College
Jackson

The William Atkinson Hall Information and Technology Center (ITC) is the foundation for a new renaissance at the college's campus, and is the result of an innovative approach to multiple academic programs resulting in a new hybrid building. The design success-fully creates a strong individual presence for the ITC without disrupting the fabric of the campus. Playing off of the courtyards and site lines of existing buildings, the structure features a continuous hem that begins as a retaining wall in the entry court and folds up to a canopy wrapping around the building, ultimately becoming the roof of the two-story information commons. The building is the academic center for the college and provides state-of-the-art services to the community.

PROJECT FACTS

Address: 2111 Emmons Road, Jackson, MI 49201, USA. **Client:** Jackson Community College.
Completion: 2007. **Size:** 4,923 m².

↑ | **Façade**
← | **Interior,** Service Desk
↗ | **Interior,** Collaboratorium
→ | **Interior,** Information Commons

↑ | **Pine Jog Garden**
→ | **Eco trail**

Pine Jog Elementary School
Palm Beach

Consisting of a K–5 Elementary School and an Environmental Education Center, the project is a one of a kind joint-use public school campus, which is the first in Florida to achieve LEED gold certification. The facilities' mission is to inspire and excite children and residents to become responsible citizens. This project represents a new paradigm of school design; the curriculum combines traditional education with comprehensive ecological awareness by synergizing the programs, building systems, and design features of the two adjacent facilities, limiting impact to the site and the community. The buildings and site are designed to help teachers teach and students learn, while reducing long-term operational costs.

PROJECT FACTS
Address: 6315 Summit Blvd., East Palm Beach, FL 33415, USA. **Client:** The School District of Palm Beach County. **Completion:** 2008. **Size:** 11,918 m².

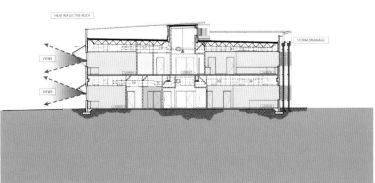

↑ | Section
↖ | Siteplan
← | EcoPorch
↙ | Classroom
↓ | Exterior view

habermann.stock.decker.
architects

↑ | **Schoolyard**
→ | **Staircase**

Erwin-Teufel-Schule
Spaichingen

In the design concept, a newly created access road from the main street in the north to the lower parking lots in the south acts as a unifying, and at the same time dividing, element. The road transverses the vocational schools and adivides the building into its functional modules – the two-floor workshop building in the west and the three-floor theory building in the east. Schoolyards, staircases and seating steps constitute usable elements of this road. Similarly, the entrance hall is not a building structure but rather a section of the traversing road. A stairway with seating stairs connects the different entrance levels of the lounge, while its stairs invite passersby to sit down and relax.

PROJECT FACTS

Address: Alleenstrasse 40, 78549 Spaichingen, Germany. **Client:** Municipality of Tuttlingen.
Completion: 2005. **Size:** 10,132 m².

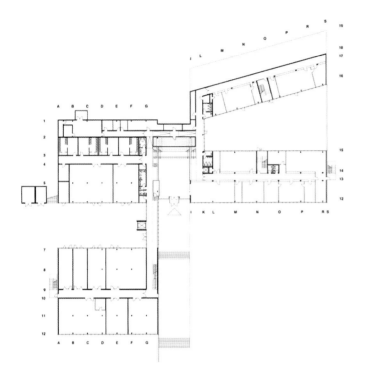

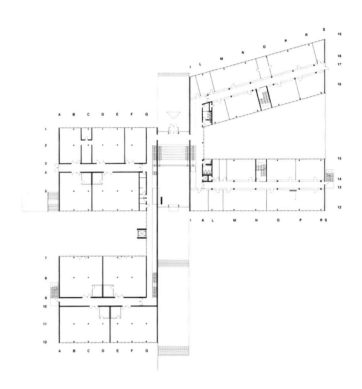

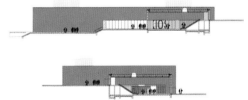

↖↖ | Entrance
←← | Hall
↖ | Floor plans
↑ | Sections
← | Interior view

Exam

↑ | **External view**
→ | **Internal view**

Expansion Primary School
Steinmürli

The new solitaire marks the south bondary of the schoolyard. Old gym and new gym form a new yard, due to their orthogonal positions. Both cubes are integrated by shape and color into the existing facility, they receive their special contemporary expression through the surfaces of conrete elements and the perforated front of the vent wings. In the upper floors of the classroom building, the classrooms are grouped ring-shaped around the large lobby. The lobby will be illuminated by areaways. Haptic façades, clean design and transparency give the school a playful and open expression.

PROJECT FACTS

Address: Römerstrasse 13, 8953 Dietikon, Switzerland. **Client:** City of Dietikon. **Completion:** 2006.
Size: 3,200 m². **Grades:** 1–3.

← | Areaway
↓ | Section
↙ | Floor plan
→ | Night view
↘ | View to the entrance

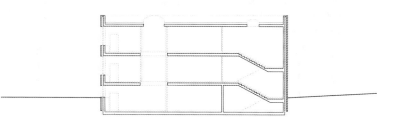

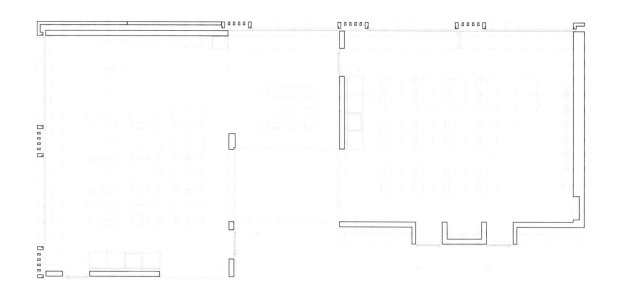

gpy arquitectos

↑ I **Exterior view**
→ I **Interior view**

Tenerife School of Dramatic Arts

Santa Cruz de Tenerife

The building is presented as a great dais, an urban stage with the city and the landscape as a backdrop, a public forum where the actors are the city-dwellers and the island plays the role of background scenery. A dais which has been removed from its usual context – the codified theater building – and brought closer to the elements of everyday life: the street, the city, the mountains and the sea. In the initial sketches, a rectangular platform linked to the horizon harked back to the origins of theater: as an open yet limited space, directly linked to nature.Like a huge stage set, moved by some oceanic theater machinery, the island of Gran Canaria rises up on the horizon like a prop to be used for this particular scene: boats, islands, mountains, clouds.

PROJECT FACTS
Address: Calle Pedro Suárez Hernández s/n, El Ramonal, 38009 Santa Cruz de Tenerife, Spain.
Client: Canary Islands Government. **Completion:** 2003. **Size:** 3,360 m².

← | **Wall**, detail
↓ | **Section, floor plan, sketch**
→ | **Gym**
↘ | **Performance**

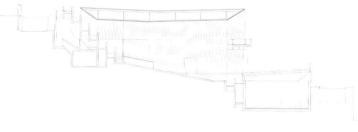

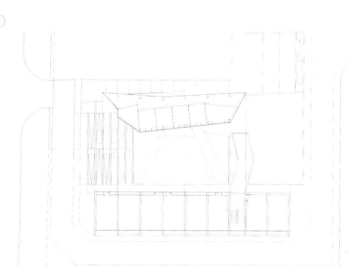

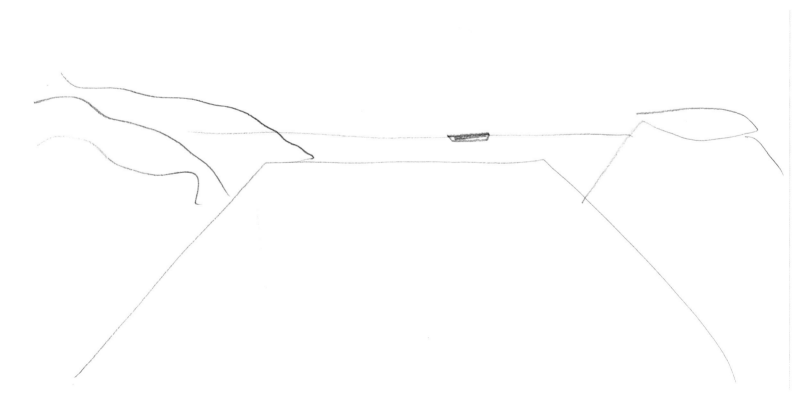

dl-a
designlab architecture

↑ | **External corner**
→ | **Nightshot**

Lucciole

Cressy

The school center and the bus shelter are positioned in the middle of a new ensemble of residential buildings. The project design underlines the special nature of these public facilities. The three buildings are set apart by a series of geometrical circles that create intermediate spaces, which open onto each other. Each of the three "objects" is positioned on a plateau of brushed concrete (a larger squared structure for the school, a small cubic structure for the activity building, and a long semi-buried structure for the gymnasium) and is enveloped by a double glass skin for rational heat exchange management. The accumulated energy lights up this double skin at night. Resembling fireflies, their fluorescence epitomizes the playful character of this public space.

PROJECT FACTS

Address: Rue Edouard-Vallet 16–18, 1232 Cressy, Switzerland. **Client:** Municipality of Bernex and Confignon. **Completion:** 2006. **Size:** 6,042 m². **School type:** primary school. **Grades:** 1–6.

←←| Façade with curtains
↙↙| View without curtains
← | Internal view
↙ | Staircase
↓ | Sections
↓↓| Floor plan

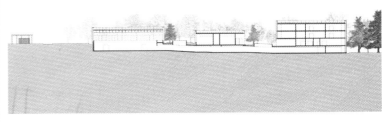

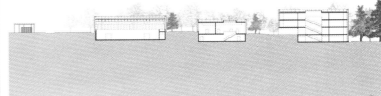

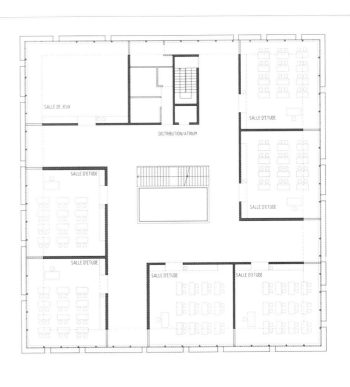

Klein & Sänger

↑ | **External view**
→ | **Façade**, detail

Gymnasium Bruckmühl
Bruckmühl

The U-shaped school building is accessible from the narrow eastern side. Above the entrance, which opens to an atrium, there are management and staff room. Classrooms can be found on the other side, facing south with a view to the nearby Alps, the music and drawing classes are facing north. A glass bridge connects the different parts of the building in the West. Depending on the energetic and climatic needs, all four façades are structured differently. The reinforced concrete bulkheads are used to heat storage, the location of the rooms and the arrangement of ventilation flaps and double sliding windows allow a manual regulation. The central hall is equipped with a photovoltaic roof.

PROJECT FACTS

Address: Kirchdorfer Strasse 21, 83832 Bruckmühl, Germany. **Client:** Municipality of Rosenheim.
Completion: 2003. **Size:** 10,800 m². **Grades:** 5–12.

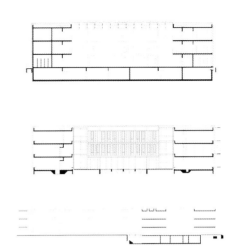

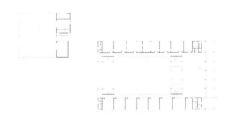

↑ | Sections, floor plan
↖ | Classroom
←↙ | Hall, gym
↓ | Schoolyard

Bünzli & Courvoisier
Architekten

↑ | External view
→ | Façade

School Building Oelwiese
Thalwil

The materials used for the new building clearly identify it as a contemporary building. It mainly consists of a compact concrete structure whose interior room division is visible from the outside. This double-layer construction increases the thermal insulation of the façade, protects the interior wooden windows, and provides a weather-proof sun screen. The exterior is dominated by the multiple façade layers. The wooden windows are perceptible behind the exterior glazing, adding warmth to the protective glass cover. As opposed to the façade, which strongly affects the interior atmosphere, sparse materials were used inside with plastered walls and ceilings and floors covered in concrete.

PROJECT FACTS **Address:** Wiesenstrasse 19, 8800 Thalwil, Switzerland. **Client:** Municipality of Thalwil. **Completion:** 2009. **Size:** 900 m² (new) and 890 m² (old). **School type:** primary school.

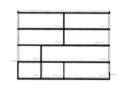

↖ | Hall, floor plan, section, site plan
← | Front view
↗ | Classroom
→ | Classroom

AMELLER, DUBOIS
& ASSOCIÉS

↑ | **Exterior view**
→ | **Interior view**

Lycée Louis Armand

Eaubonne

Behind the perforated aluminum-clad façade a 10,000 square meter atrium with a height
of three storeys can be found. All three floors have their own colors dedicated to. The
colors meet again in the atrium and form a work of art in the style of Mondrian. The architects have managed to establish a connection between old and new building to enable
a stable educational work.

PROJECT FACTS
Address: 32, Rue Stéphane Proust. 95600 Eaubonne, France. **Client:** Municipality of Île-de-France.
Completion: 2007. **Size:** 10,000 m².

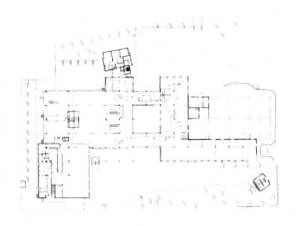

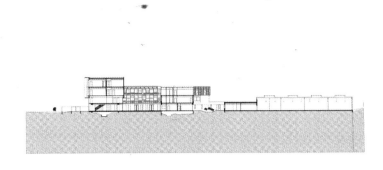

↖ | Floor plan, section
← | Atrium
↙ | Interior view
↓ | Classroom

↑ | Exterior view
→ | Areaway

Elementary School Schulzendorf

Schulzendorf

The basic shape of the existing building is that of an <H> with two yards opening up to the outside. The extension closes the <H> on both sides into a figure <8>. The open yards are turned into interior glazed atriums surrounded by the old and new classroom areas. A seamless cover on top of the existing building and the two extensions turns old and new into a single body. The linking material is a suspended rear-ventilated façade made of locally plated willow. The color concept focuses on the public areas. Each floor and each atrium has its own color. The monochrome colors extend across floors and ceilings, creating rooms specifically created for children.

PROJECT FACTS
Address: Illgenstrasse 26–32, 15732 Schulzendorf, Germany. **Client:** Municipality of Schulzendorf. **Other creatives involvedddress:** Guido Neubeck. **Completion:** 2006.

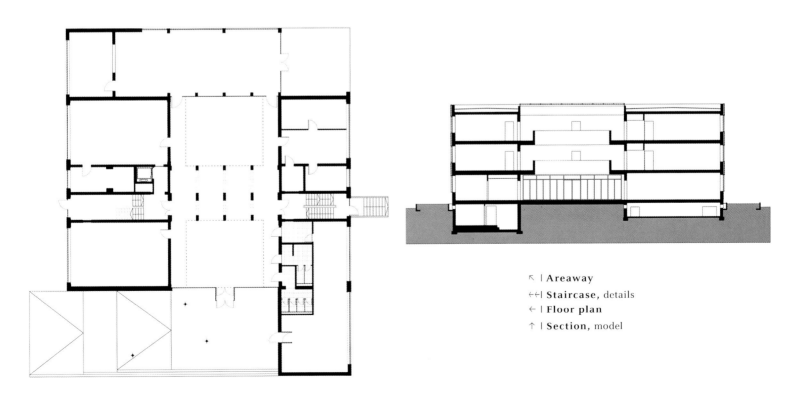

↖ | **Areaway**
←←| **Staircase**, details
← | **Floor plan**
↑ | **Section**, model

plus+bauplanung GmbH

↑ | **Night view**
→ | **Green marketplace**

Protestant Comprehensive School
Gelsenkirchen-Bismarck

School is the most formative environment for children, it should be their second home,
appeal to all senses and be a place that they enjoy attending. The acceptance, understanding and tender care for buildings and cities is based on their individual nature. The comprehensive school is located in an underprivileged district of the Ruhr region in Germany.
The district became a place of learning while the school was integrated into the city with
a municipal hall, theater, library and gymnasium. Six row housing units are located on
six side streets. They each contain one school grade with five individual classes, which
remain in "their" buildings for their entire schooling.

Adress: Laarstrasse 41, 45889 Gelsenkirchen-Bismarck, Germany. **Client:** Protestant School in Westfalia e.V.
Completion: 2004. **Size:** 16,000 m². **School type:** comprehensive school. **Grades:** 5–10.

↑ | General view
↙ | Sitepan, sections
↗ | Schoolyard
→ | Auditorium

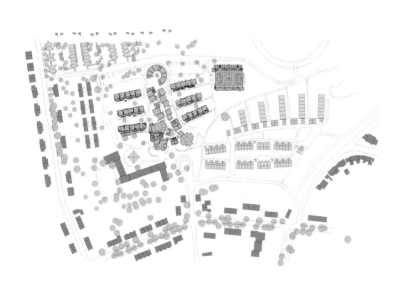

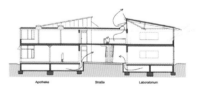

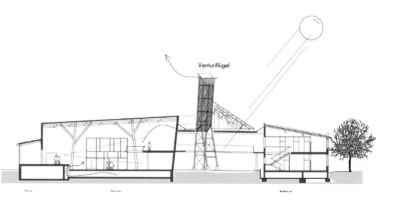

Rémy Marciano

↑ | **Exterior view**
→ | **Façade**

IUFM - Formation des Maîtres

La Seyne sur Mer

The IUFM is Rémy Marciono's second work in la Seyne sur Mer. The sites and activities of shipbuilding are still present in the heart and concerns of the Seynois people. They created the image of the city, they are local heritage, cultural heritage. By its architecture, the IUFM summarizes a set of codes of identity which are associated with this heritage. The façade randomly assembled of plates, reminds us of the construction of ship hulls as well as the red brick colors do remind us of factory buildings. Thus, a factory or even dockyard for teachers had been created by the architect.

PROJECT FACTS

Address: Boulevard Toussaint Merle, 83500 La Seyne sur Mer, France. **Client:** Municipality of Région Provence Alpes Cote d'Azur, Mandataire AREA. **Completion:** 2004.

↖ | **Front view**
← | **Side view**
↑ | **Façade**, detail
↓ | **Site plan**

REPORT C

COURSE TEACHER	0	NC
READING-	1	
ENGLISH		2
SOC		
BAND		

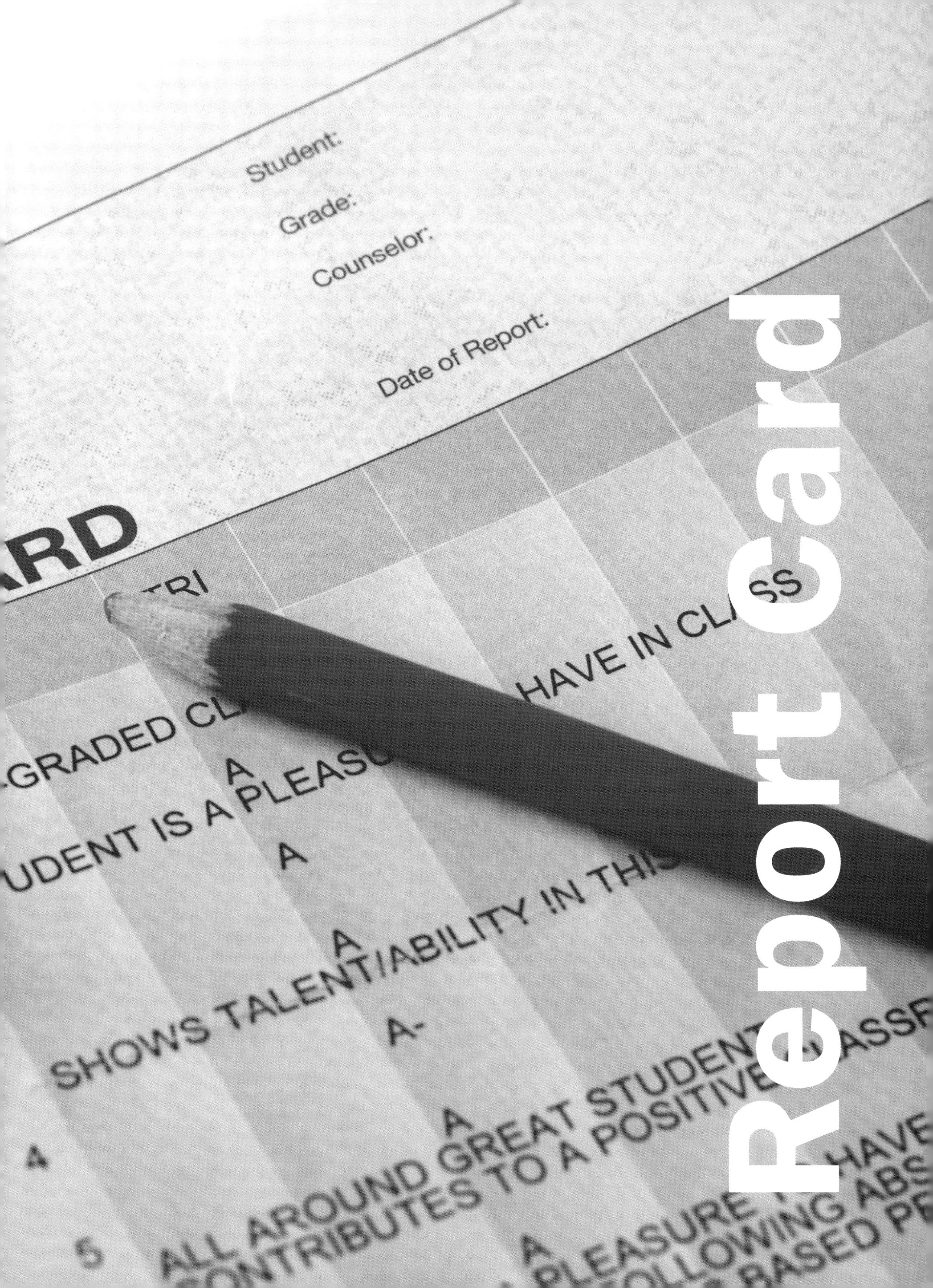

Report Card

RD

Student:

Grade:

Counselor:

Date of Report:

TRI

HAVE IN CLASS

GRADED CL

A

UDENT IS A PLEAS

A

SHOWS TALENT/ABILITY IN THIS

A

A-

4

A

ALL AROUND GREAT STUDENT

CONTRIBUTES TO A POSITIVE CLASSR

5

PLEASURE

FOLLOWING ABS

BASED PE

Anna Heringer, Mag. arch.
Eike Roswag,
Dipl. Ing. Architekt

↑ | **Interior view**, cave
→ | **Exterior view**, corner

School Handmade in Bangladesh
Rudrapur

The entire project includes the building of a school as a representative public building, the building of two-story houses as a model for rural living as well as the design of the outside areas. The ultimate goal is to gain and disseminate knowledge and information for optimising the use of locally available resources. The improvement of the building techniques is as important as the economic aspects and the creation of a regional identity. In order to create jobs and to build up a capacity for producing sustainable architecture it is essential to include local workers in the building process. Training through "learning by doing" should help the local craftsmen to improve the standards and condition of the rural housing in general.

PROJECT FACTS
Address: Rudrapur, Dinajpur, Bangladesh. **Client:** Dipshikha / METI (Modern Education and Training Institute). **Completion:** 2005. **Size:** 325 m².

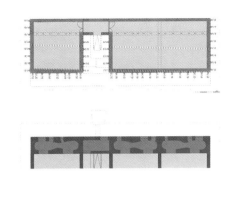

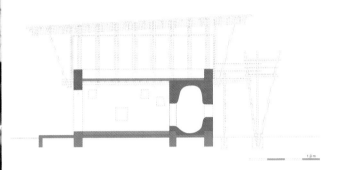

← | Front view
↙ | Classroom ground floor
↖ | Pupils in the schoolyard
↑ | Floor plan, section
↓ | Classroom first floor

Maryann Thompson
Architects

↑ | **Playground**
→ | **Staircase**

The Atrium School

Watertown

The Atrium school looked to Maryann Thompson Architects to design a facility that called for the adaptive reuse of an open warehouse structure on a limited site in a densely populated area. The oblong site presented specific challenges including how best to arrange parking fields, accommodate green space, and orchestrate pedestrian and vehicular traffic through the site. The school's entrance and vehicular access was repositioned to the back of the campus away from the building's prior entrance, which faced a main thoroughfare. Extensive glazing and skylights brightened the previously dark and enclosed warehouse space and also facilitated cross-ventilation. The double loaded corridor was enlivened with special window nooks, which provide moments of rest and discovery and an unfolding spatial experience.

PROJECT FACTS
Address: 69 Grove Street, Watertown, MA 02472, USA. **Completion:** 2006. **Size:** 2,323 m².
School type: private / early education. **Grades:** kindergarden to grade 6.

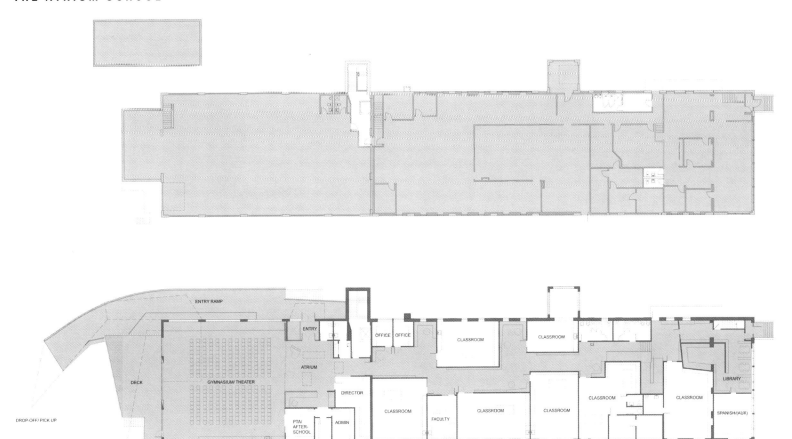

ENTRY RAMP

DROP-OFF/ PICK UP

DECK

GYMNASIUM/ THEATER

ATRIUM

ENTRY

OFFICE OFFICE

CLASSROOM

CLASSROOM

DIRECTOR

PTA/ AFTER-SCHOOL

ADMIN

CLASSROOM

FACULTY

CLASSROOM

CLASSROOM

CLASSROOM

CLASSROOM

LIBRARY

SPANISH/(AUX)

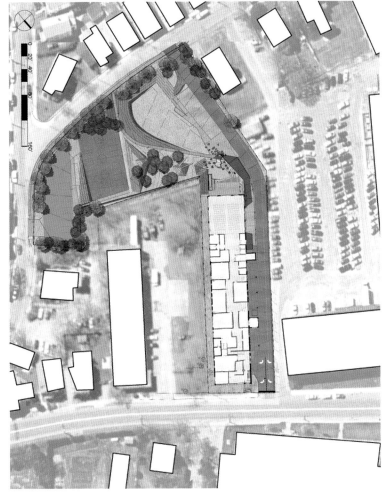

↖↖ | **Exterior view**

↖ | **Learning spaces**

←← | **New entrance to school**

↑↑ | **Floor plan,** before

↑ | **Floor plan,** revised

← | **Site plan**

farwick + grote
architekten bda
stadtplaner

↑ | **Exterior view**, schoolyard
→ | **Façade**, detail

Upper School Schillerstraße
Berlin

The restoration of urban spaces and the compression of the internal block structure are the assumptions of the design concept. Typologically from the perimeter block buildings develops an overall structure with a large, open courtyard, which forms together with the forum and the cafeteria the middle of the school. The different components give the school a reasonable public appearance and unique identity. Natural materials such as larch and Anröchter dolomite create a good learning atmosphere. The combination of profiled, yellow bricks and colored concrete elements create a powerful materiality of the façade.

PROJECT FACTS

Address: Schillerstrasse 121, 10625 Berlin, Germany. **Client:** Municipality of Berlin. **Completion:** 2008. **Size:** **11,000** m². **Grades:** 10–13.

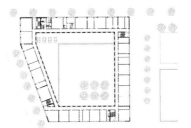

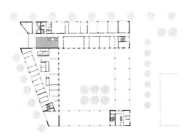

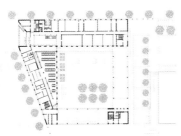

←← | Schoolyard
↙ | Staircase
‹ | Floor plans, site plan
↓ | Interior view

schulz & schulz

↑ | **Interior view**
→ | **Façade**, detail

Extension of Neue Nikolaischule
Leipzig

A multi-purpose hall to be used as an auditorium and gymnasium was added to the early
20th century Neue Nikolaischule building in Leipzig. The new building reflects the cubic
style of the former boys' gymnasium, which was destroyed in the war, and reproduces
the historical symmetry of the overall structure. The façade transforms the existing rustic
plaster façade of the Wilhelminian-era school through specially developed rear ventilated
plaster elements. The lathing is made of aluminum sandwich plates with a honeycomb
core. In the lateral glazing section, the plaster elements consist of loose slats. Depending
on the use of the hall, they can be used to shield or allow a free view of the outdoors.

PROJECT FACTS

Address: Schönbachstrasse 17, 04299 Leipzig, Germany. **Client:** Municipality of Leipzig. **Completion:** 2003. **Size** 750 m². **Type of school:** secondary school. **Grades:** 5–12.

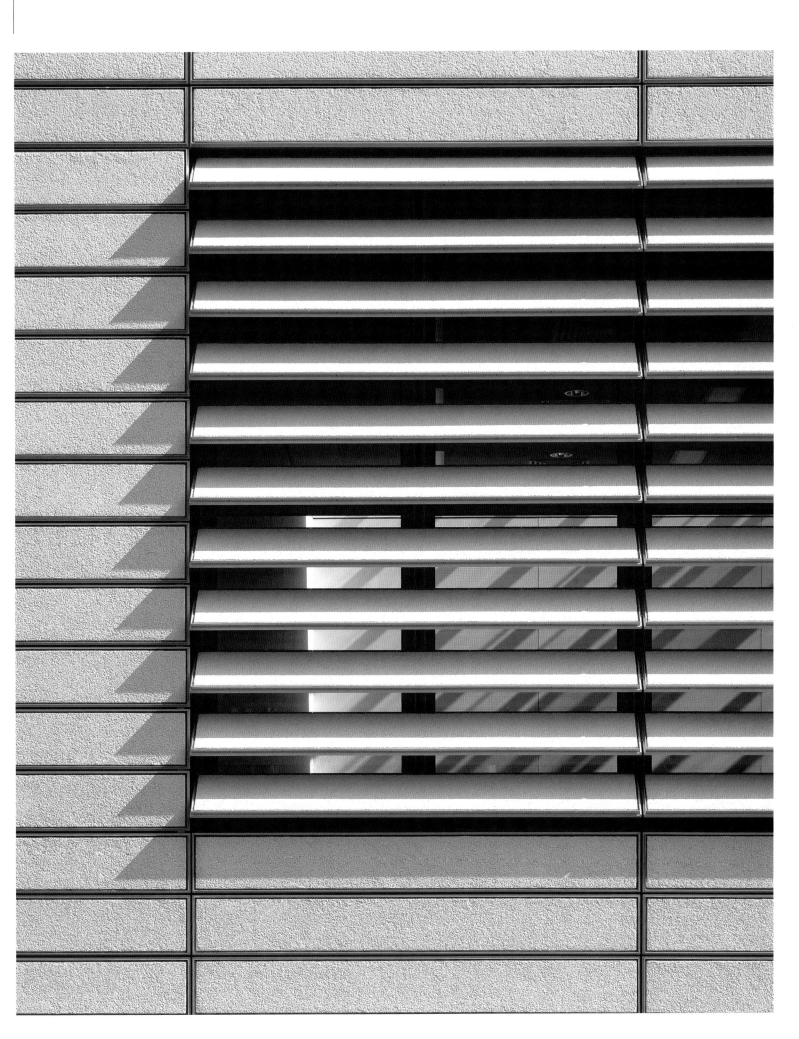

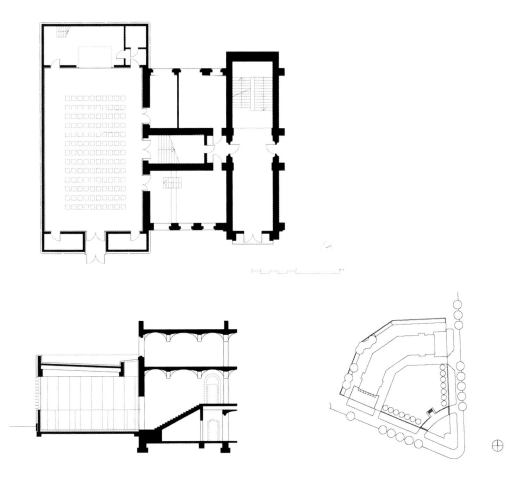

←← | **Exterior view**, day and night
↑ | **Floor plan, section, site plan**
← | **View from schoolyard**

↑ | **Bird's eye view**
→ | **Yard,** detail

Day-care Center Skanderborggade
Copenhagen

The building design is the result of the planning regulations and authorities and the call for the greatest possible connection between the outdoor areas of the ground and roof plans, and taking optimal advantage of site's sun orientation. The building consists of two planes which extend to the boundaries of the site. One plane forms the ground terrain plane covering the contaminated ground, a second forms the roof. The ground terrain surface is folded upwards in such a way that it forms a hill or slope between the ground and roof. Underneath the slope forms an unheated space where a forest of columns is used for swings and other forms of play, when the weather is cold or wet. Two other light wells cut into the roof plane ensure daylight and a variety of outdoor space in conjunction with the other rooms of the building.

PROJECT FACTS

Address: Krausegade 17, 2100 Copenhagen, Denmark. **Client:** Municipality of Copenhagen.
Completion: 2005. **Size:** 555 m² (floorage), 490 m² (outdoor area).

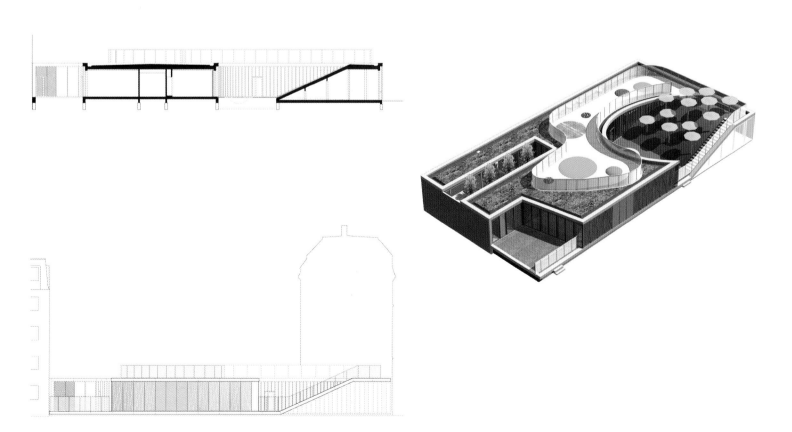

← | **Overall view**
↓ | **Floor plan**
↖ | **Exterior,** corner
↙ | **Sections, model sketch**

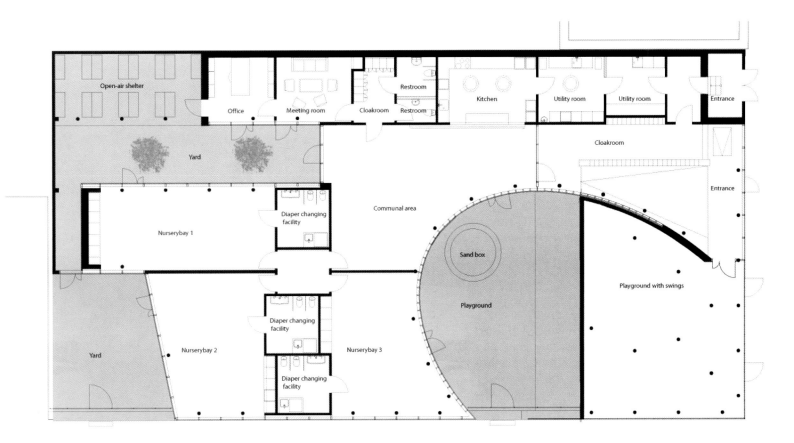

Open-air shelter

Office

Meeting room

Cloakroom

Restroom

Restroom

Kitchen

Utility room

Utility room

Entrance

Cloakroom

Entrance

Yard

Communal area

Diaper changing facility

Nurserybay 1

Sand box

Playground

Playground with swings

Diaper changing facility

Yard

Nurserybay 2

Diaper changing facility

Nurserybay 3

Graber Pulver Architekten

↑ | External view
→ | Façade

School Foundation Glarisegg
Steckborn

The project incorporates three residential buildings for three groups of adolescents with supervising tutors and caretakers. Complementing the medieval main building, the angled shape of the one to two-floor building creates an exterior space with access from the lakeside and a garden in the south. The rooms are grouped in three residential units and divide the open, commonly used living, dining and play area. Numerous, diagonal room relations provide all units with views of the other residential groups, the lake, and the garden. The wooden façade is reminiscent of rural sheds or simple accommodations such as youth hostels.

PROJECT FACTS

Address: Schulstiftung Glarisegg, 8266 Steckborn, Switzerland. **Client:** Schulstiftung Glarisegg, Steckborn. **Completion:** 2007. **Size:** 2,048 m². **Grades:** age 7–16.

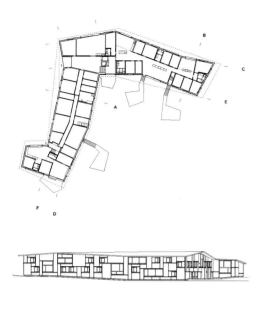

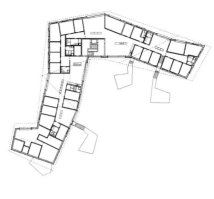

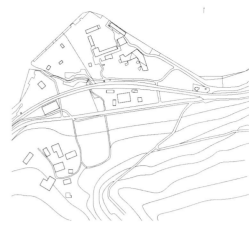

↑ | Floor plans, sections, siteplan
← | Exterior view
→ | Interior view

Lussi + Halter Partner AG

↑ | **Front view**
→ | **Façade**, detail

School Building Dreilinden
Luzern

The floor plan consists of a dynamic path enhancing the inner life of the classrooms and especially the areas in between. It extends spirally from the basement to the surrounding galleries and gymnasium side rooms to the entrance floor with the inner courtyard, the assembly hall, and cafeteria terrace. The path culminates in the upper floors where the information technology and classrooms offer a view of the city and surrounding landscape. Three materials dominate the building interior-concrete on walls and ceilings, light beige colored natural stone on the floors of the hallways, the public areas, and the cafeteria, and oak on the classroom floors, furniture, doors, cladding and windows.

PROJECT FACTS
Address: Dreilindenstrasse 20, 6006 Luzern, Switzerland. **Client:** Kaufmännischer Verband Luzern.
Completion: 2005. **Size:** 5,800 m². **School type:** training school.

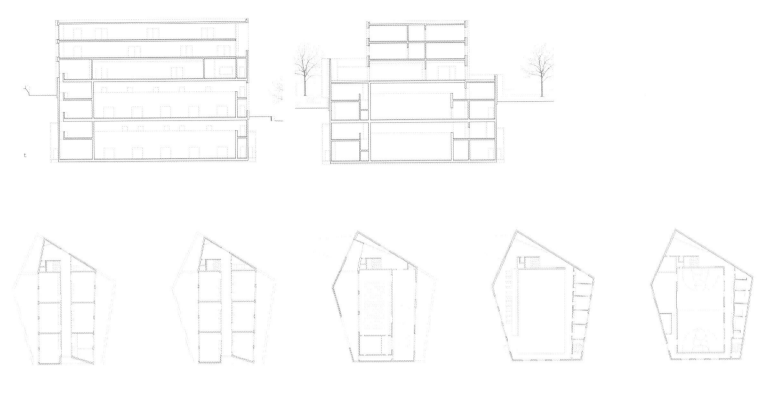

← | Gym
↙ | Rear view
↖ | Sections and floor plans
↓ | Window to the cemetery

↑ | **Exterior view**
→ | **Schoolyard**

Het 4e Gymnasium

Amsterdam

In 2008 HVDN architects designed the building for the 4e Gymnasium of Amsterdam. This modular building is located in the Houthavens: an area that due to problems with the development-zoning plan is temporarily in use. Because of a number of innovations the building is not only movable, it also has got both on technically and aesthetic area the qualities and a level of finishing which is similar to permanent traditional construction. The 4,100 square meters school building was completed in 6 month and is characterizes by expressive colors and a smart routing.

PROJECT FACTS **Address:** Stavangerweg 902, 1013 AX Amsterdam, The Netherlands. **Client:** Stadsdeel Westerpark Amsterdam. **Completion:** 2008. **Size:** 4,160 m².

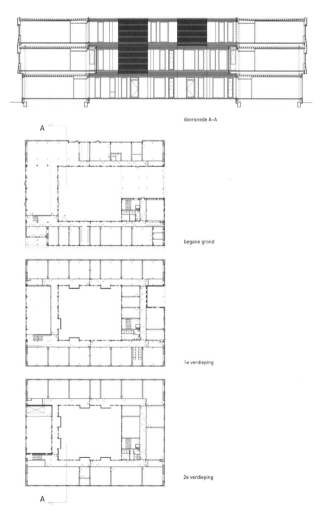

doorsnede A-A

begane grond

1e verdieping

2e verdieping

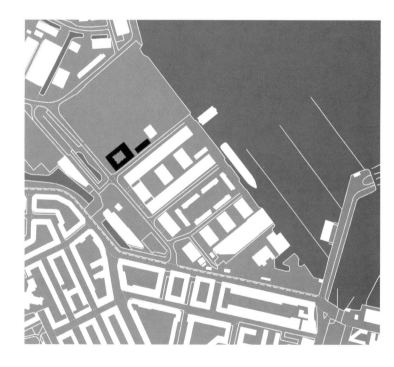

↖ | Schoolyard
← | Sections, floor plans
↑ | Site plan
↗↗ | Hall with view to yard
→ | Interior view

↑ I **Exterior view,** façade
→ I **Staircase**

Transformation School and Gym

Renens

The two existing buildings were rather disparate. The new project creates a link between them, in particular with the new façade design. Neutrally colored, a double-insulated façade made of zinc-titanium with fixed colored sunshades wraps both buildings, creating an optical connection. The sunshades in front of the school buildings keep the outside visible from the inside, and their colors are also incorporated into the interior design. The shades in front of the gymnasium provide visual and sun protection.

PROJECT FACTS
Address: Chemin de la Roche, 1020 Renens, Vaud, Switzerland. **Client:** Municipality of Renens.
Completion: 2008. **Size:** 3,044 m² (school) , 765 m²(gym).

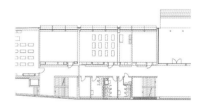

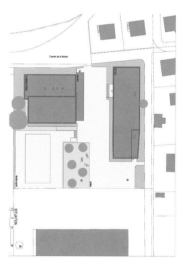

↖ | **Façade**, detail
↑ | **Floor plans**
← | **Gym**
↗ | **Schoolyard**
→ | **Classroom**

School´s Out

JSWD Architekten

↑ | **Bird's eye view**
→ | **Rendering**

École Centrale Clausen

Luxembourg

The City of Luxembourg is planning an elementary school and kindergarten including a gymnasium for the city's quarter of Clausen, located in the valley of Alzette. The two buildings clasp around a rectangular clearance, which forms the center point of the facility. Only a relatively small, sloping space came into question due to the constriction resulting from the river valley. It was this situation that fostered the idea of an ensemble that correlates with the topography of the location. The buildings and school courtyard thus group across several levels. The sports hall is embedded into the slope and the topmost level of the school courtyard spans across its roof. This interaction of buildings with urban motifs such as alley, street and space allow for inspiring moments to develop. Two wide stairways bridge the difference in height between the Alzet river bank and the higher levels.

PROJECT FACTS **Address:** 42, place Guillaume II, 2090 Luxembourg. **Client:** Municipality of Luxembourg. **Completion:** 2011. **Size:** 4,000 m². **School type:** primary school. **Grades:** 1–6.

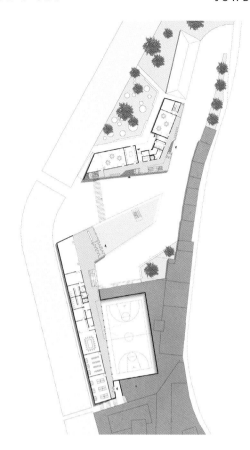

↑ | **Site plans**, ground floor and first floor
→ | **Section**, view from the south
↘ | **Drawings**

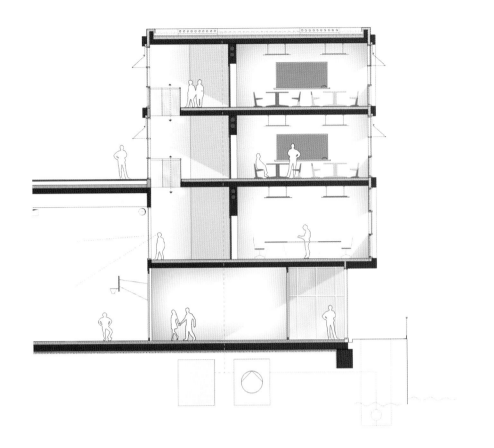

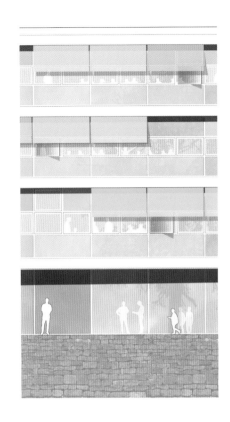

↑ I **Exterior view**
→ I **Façade**, detail

Hilde-Domin-Schule

Herrenberg

The original school complex for domestic economics and agriculture designed by Behnisch & Partner was completed in 1983. In 2004 Behnisch Architekten were commissioned to design a new, independently accessible annex that was to function autonomously. The new building is sited immediately to the south of the original accommodating six craft workshops and two classrooms with ancillary rooms, a small assembly hall, offices for staff and the pupils' council, a doctor's surgery and a room for meetings with parents. Classrooms and workshops are extensively glazed to both the façade and corridors creating airy, open perspectives, promoting visual contact between the school community and allowing natural light to flood the inner circulation areas.

PROJECT FACTS
Address: Längenholz 8, 71083 Herrenberg, Germany. **Client:** Municipality of Böblingen. **Completion:** 2007. **Size:** 1,200 m². **School type:** school for domestic economics and agriculture.

↑ | Interior view
← | Hall
↗ | Section
↗ | Exterior view
→ | Floor plan

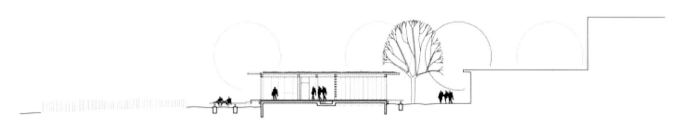

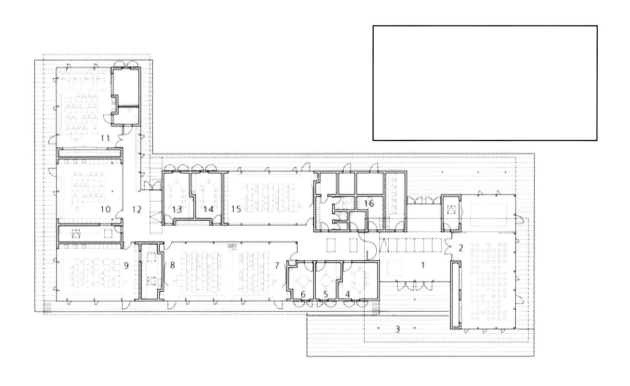

plus+bauplanung GmbH

↑ | **Exterior view**
→ | **Façade,** detail

Internationale Friedensschule
Cologne-Widdersdorf

Internationale Friedensschule Köln combines two types of schools – an international school and a multilingual high school. This basic educational concept shapes the room concept. The rooms for one international and one national class each are located next to each other, separated by a mobile partition wall. The joint hallway for each class level is divided into work areas, offering enough space for various activities. Direct emergency exits allow the implementation of this concept. The interior design is very flexible (mobile furniture, transparent walls, flexible blackboards, kitchen rows). In future construction segments, the class areas will be linked by the house of silence, the gymnasium and the theater.

PROJECT FACTS

Address: Neue Sandkaul 29, 50859 Cologne, Germany. **Client:** Amand Prima Colonia Immobilien GmbH & Co KG. **Completion:** 2009 (ongoing). **Size:** 11,570m². **Grades:** 1–12.

241

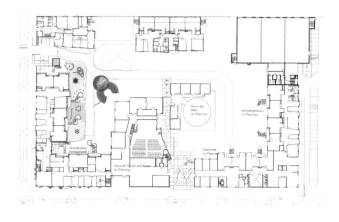

← | **Staircase**
↑ | **Floor plan, section**
↙ | **Model**
→ | **Interior view**
↘ | **Working niche,** drawing

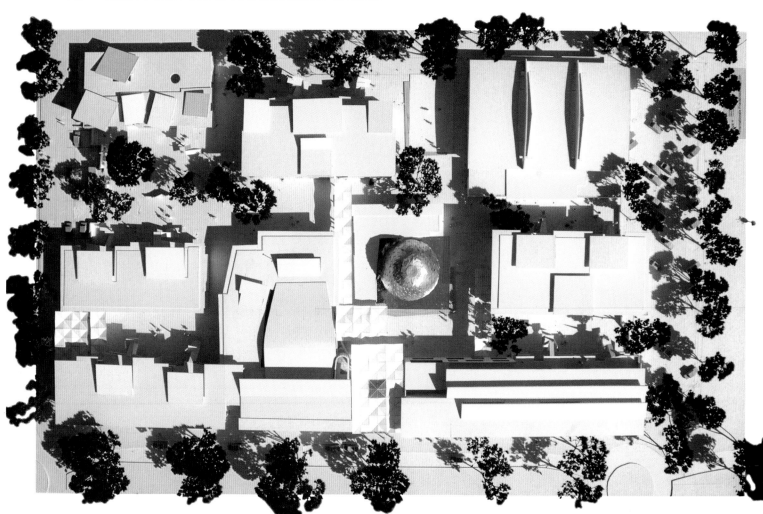

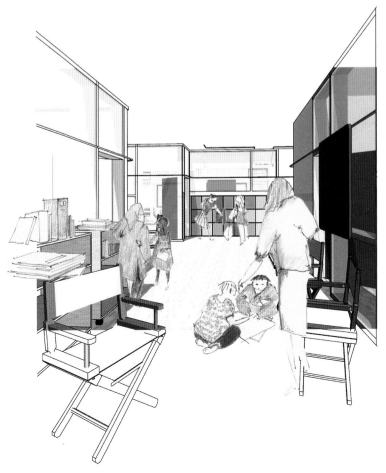

↑ | **Exterior entry court**
→ | **Interior lobby**

Lansing Community College
Lansing

The University Center is the physical embodiment of the partnership between the college and select four-year institutions, pursuing the common goal of expanding access to advanced degrees. The design of a simple form and scale contrast the various expressions surrounding the site. The program allowed the Center to connect to the historic Carnegie Library creating a marriage of architectural styles. With this opportunity, the new Center used its grandfather's stone banding in a simple concrete cantilever, which defines and shelters the main entry. The Center provides a sustainable environment and a dynamic edge to the campus, resulting in an identity for the college's partnership with the university community and space for students.

PROJECT FACTS

Address: 21 W. Shiawassee, Lansing, MI 48901, USA. **Client:** Lansing Community College.
Completion: 2007. **Size:** 3,530 m².

← | **Facde**, detail
↓ | **Information desk**
→ | **Interior**, Lobby

Fanning / Howey
Associates, Inc.

↑ | **Bright colors**
→ | **Exterior view**

Henson Valley Montessori School
Upper Marlboro

A fast-track renovation project – completed on a budget of thousands, not millions – turned a former strategic command compound into a campus for the Henson Valley Montessori School. Global themes developed for each building, and represented by flag-shaped flooring patterns and glass block coloring, honor the 35 nationalities of students and faculty. Glass block installations in the hallways display colorful patterns representing flowers, rainbows, and nature. Early childhood classrooms open to outside decks where students care for flowers, vegetable gardens, and fruit trees. A wireless network connects the senior school's four cottages, allowing students to engage in self-directed activities on the campus grounds.

PROJECT FACTS

Address: 13400 Edgemead Road, Upper Marlboro, MD 20772, USA. **Client:** Henson Valley Montessori School. **Completion:** 2007. **Size:** 3,100 m². **School type:** Montessori school.

↑ | Classroom
← | Glass block wall
↗ | Floor plan
→ | Floor plan

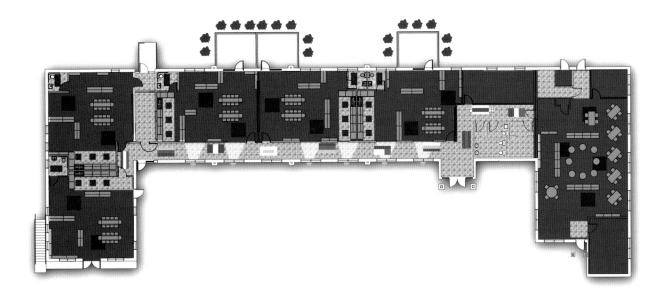

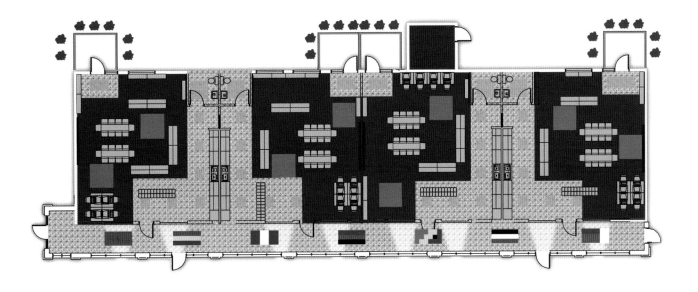

↑ | **Exterior view**
→ | **Façade**, detail

School Building Haltenstrasse
Niederscherli

The small elementary school is located in a rural residential area. The building divides the length of the slope into an upper garden section and a lower asphalt courtyard. On the village side, an extension with large windows highlights the unobstructed view from the classrooms. Underneath, the façade is rough, made of coarsely stacked concrete with hole-like cut out windows. In contrast, on the garden side the building appears loosely structured, porous and stacked. A supported marquee creates a weather-proof space in front of the entrances, acting as a visual filter between the green of the layered garden and the upper floor glazed corridor in front of the classrooms.

PROJECT FACTS

Address: Schulhaus Haltenstrasse, 3145 Niederscherli, Switzerland. **Client:** Municipality of Köniz. **Other creatives involved:** Arno Hassler, Crémines. **Completion:** 2005. **Size:** 1,547 m². **School type:** elementary school with kindergarden.

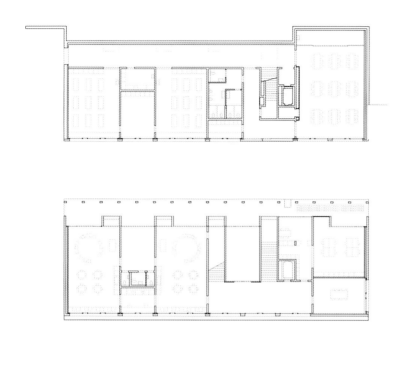

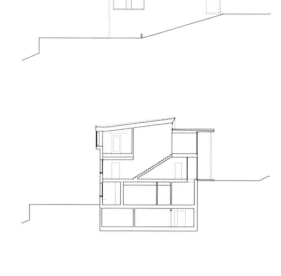

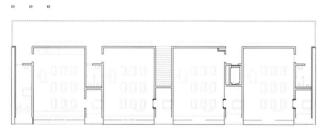

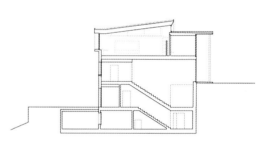

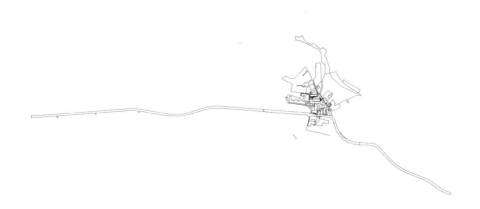

↖ | **Floor plans, sections, siteplan**
→ | **Hall**

_BOEGLI_KRAMP
ARCHITEKTEN AG

↑ | **Exterior view**
→ | **Façade and schoolyard**

Intercantonal High School

Broye region, Payerne

The school is located on the outskirts of Payerne, capital town of the Broye Region in the canton of Vaud. Considering the complexity and range of purpose and function contained within the school, the campus calls to mind a small, self-contained urban environment. The enormous amount of space is arranged in a sickle-shaped block made up of a series of buildings. The main entrances from a long central court close the building in on itself while generous apertures open the court to the landscape. The upper ground floor contains the administrative offices, library and restaurant. The 70 classrooms are situated on the other three ground floors. At both ends of the building the assembly hall and the three-court gymnasium complete the volume.

PROJECT FACTS
Address: Rue du gymnase 1, 1530 Payerne, Switzerland. **Client:** Cantons of Freiburg and Waadt.
Completion: 2005. **Size:** 22,000 m². **Grades:** 9–12.

↖ | **Floor plan, sections**
↑ | **Classroom**
↗ | **Hall**
→ | **Schoolyard**

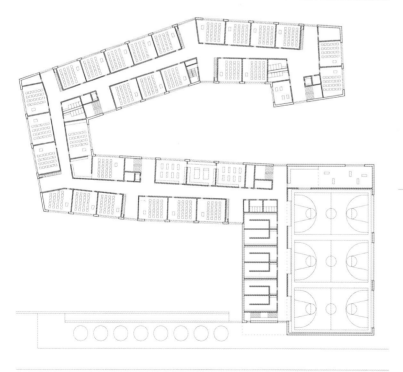

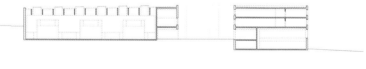

schulz & schulz

↑ | **External view**
↗ | **Staircase**, detail

Boarding School of Music
Dresden

The urban planning concept consists of two independent boarding school buildings that resemble the typical villas of the setting. The cubic houses are positioned cross-wise to each other and in relation to the existing British oak tree, a natural monument that dominates the park premises. The layout is based on a residential group concept – two students share a room, four students share a bath with a dressing area, and all eight students of a floor get together in a shared recreational lounge located at the heart of the square layout aligned with the old oak tree.

PROJECT FACTS

Address: Mendelssohnallee 34, 01309 Dresden-Blasewitz, Germany. **Client:** Municipality of Saxony, SIB.
Completion: 2008. **Size:** 1,800 m².

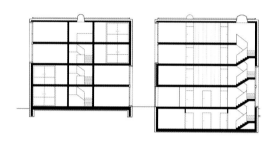

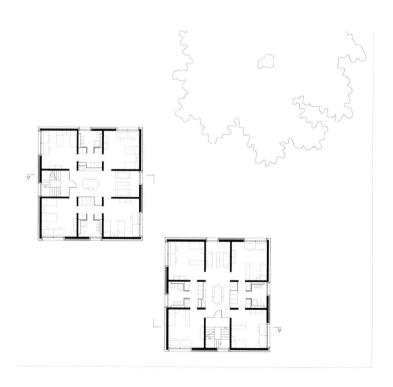

↑ | Site plan, sections, floor plan
↙ | Exterior view
↗ | Façade
→ | Room

Index

3XN A/S

Strandgade 73, 3.
1401 Copenhagen (Denmark)
T +45 7026 2648
F +45 7026 2649
3xn@3xn.dk
www.3xn.com

→28

Aeschlimann Prêtre Hasler Architekten

Räffelstrasse 11
8045 Zurich (Switzerland)
T +43 33 33 900
F +43 33 33 919
aph@aph-arch.ch
www.aph-architekten.ch

→32

Allmann Sattler Wappner Architekten

Nymphenburger Strasse 125
80636 Munich (Germany)
T +49 89 139925 0
F +49 89 139925 99
info@allmannsattlerwappner.de
www.allmannsattlerwappner.de

→16

AMELLER, DUBOIS & ASSOCIÉS

8, impasse druinot
75012 Paris (France)
T +33 153 17 17 19
F +33 153 17 18 83
contact@ameller-dubois.fr
www.ameller-dubois.fr

→176

atelier PRO

Kerkhoflaan 11A
2585 JB The Hague (The Netherlands)
T +31 70 350 69 00
F +31 70 351 49 71
info@atelierpro.nl
www.atelierpro.nl

→36, 130

Behnisch Architekten
(former: Behnisch, Behnisch & Partner)

Rotebühlstrasse 163A
70197 Stuttgart (Germany)
T +49 711 70 77 20
F +49 711 60 77 299
buero@behnisch.com
www.behnisch.com

→96, 236

BOEGLI_KRAMP ARCHITEKTEN AG

Dipl. Architekten ETH FH SIA SWB
Route de la Fonderie 8C
1700 Fribourg (Switzerland)
T +41 26 422 422 1
F +41 26 422 422 0
info@boeglikramp.ch
www.boeglikramp.ch

→256

Bünzli & Courvoisier Architekten ETH/SIA/BSA

Limmatstrasse 285
8005 Zurich (Switzerland)
T +41 44 274 10 60
F +41 44 272 10 61
mail@bcarch.ch

→172

Jean-Patrice CALORI CAB architectes

4 rue guiglia
06000 Nice (France)
T +33 4 93 16 17 57
F +33 4 93 16 91 51
agengecab@wanadoo.fr
www.agencecab.com

→88

fabio capanni workshop

Via del romito 2
50134 Florence (Italy)
T +39 055 48 49 71
F +39 055 48 49 71
studio@fabiocapanni.it
www.fabiocapanni.it

→100

CPG Consultants Pte Ltd

238B Thomson Road, #12-00 Tower B Novena Square
307685 Singapore
T +65 6357 4449
F +65 6357 4469
nina.yang@cpgcorp.com.sg
www.cpgcorp.com.sg

→92

deffner voitländer architekten bda

Gottesackerstrasse 21
85221 Dachau (Germany)
T +49 8131 27 170 0
F +49 8131 27 170 27
werkraum@dv-arc.de
www.dv-arc.de

→70

Diezinger & Kramer
Dipl.Ing. Architekten BDA

Römerstrasse 23
85072 Eichstätt (Germany)
T +49 8421 97 86 0
F +49 8421 97 86 86
architekten@diezingerkramer.de
www.diezingerkramer.de

→44

dl-a, designlab-architecture
sa. Patrick Devanthéry &
Inès Lamunière Architects

Rue du Tunnel 7
1227 Carouge/Genève (Switzerland)
T +41 22 307 01 30
F +41 22 343 05 54
mail@dl-a.ch
www.dl-a.ch

→164

Enzmann + Fischer AG Architekt/innen BSA SIA

Seebahnstrasse 109
8003 Zurich (Switzerland)
T +41 44 455 77 77
F +41 44 455 77 79
mail@enzmannfischer.ch
www.enzmannfischer.ch

→156

farwick+grote architekten bda|stadtplaner

Van-Delden-Strasse 15
48683 Ahaus (Germany)
T +49 2561 42 960
F +49 2561 42 9625
info@farwickgrote.de
www.farwickgrote.de

→202

Fanning/Howey Associates, Inc.

210 N. Lee Street, Suite 208
Alexandria, VA 22314 (USA)
T +1 703 519 9822
F +1 703 519 9823
eschmidt@fhai.com
www.fhai.com

→248

Forte, Gimenes & Marcondes Ferraz Arquitectos

Rua Mourato Coelho, 923
Vila Madalena, CEP 05417011 (Brazil)
T +55 11 303 228 26
F +55 11 303 228 26
forte@fgmf.com.br
www.fgmf.com.br

→12

FXFOWLE ARCHITECTS

22 West 19 Street, New York
NY 10011 (USA)
T +1 212 627 1700
info@fxfowle.com
www.fxfowle.com

→20

Galletti & Matter
Claude Anne-Marie Matter Galetti
architecte epfl-fas-sia

Avenue de Montoie 20 bis
1007 Lausanne (Switzerland)
T +41 21 625 04 68
F +41 21 625 04 69
gm.architectes@bluewin.ch
www.galetti-matter.ch

→76, 226

Georg Scheel Wetzel Architects

Marienstrasse 10
10117 Berlin (Germany)
T +49 30 27 57 24 70
F +49 30 27 57 24 77
buero@gsw-architekten.de
www.georgscheelwetzel.com

→84

gpy arquitectos

Calle Castillo 56, 2d
38003 Santa Cruz de Tenerife (Spain)
estudio@gpyarquitectos.com
www.gpyarquitectos.com

Graber Pulver Architekten

Sihlquai 75 / Gasstrasse 4
8005 Zurich / 3005 Bern (Switzerland)
T +41 44 381 8818 / +41 31 318 8818
F +41 44 381 8819 / +41 31 318 8819
arch@graberpulver.ch
www.graberpulver.ch

Haberland Architekten

Sentastrasse 3
12159 Berlin (Germany)
T +49 30 61 62 87 08
F +49 30 61 62 86 98
info@haberland-berlin.de
www.haberland-berlin.de

Anna Heringer Mag.arch
Eike Roswag Dipl.-Ing. Architekt

Lehrter Strasse 57 Haus IV
10557 Berlin (Germany)
T +49 30 89 73 37 73
F +49 30 89 73 37 72
anna-heringer@meti-school.de
eike-roswag@meti-school.de

HERLE + HERRLE Architekten BDA
Christoph Herle und Klemens Herrle

Sudetenlandstrasse 21
86633 Neuburg a.d. Donau (Germany)
T +49 8431 47 833
F +49 8431 40 989
info@herle-herrle.de
www.herle-herrle-architekten.de

h.s.d.architekten bda
habermann.stock.decker.

Slavertorwall 15
32657 Lemgo (Germany)
T +49 5261 7777 0
F +49 5261 7777 29
info@hsd-architekten.de
www.hsd-architekten.de

HVDN architecten

Krelis Louwenstraat 1 B28
1055 KA Amsterdam (The Netherlands)
T +31 20 688 5025
F +31 20 688 4793
info@hvdn.nl
www.hvdn.nl

JSWD Architekten

Maternusplatz 11
50996 Cologne (Germany)
T +49 221 93 555 0 0
F +49 221 93 555 0 55
info@jswd-architekten.de
www.jswd-architekten.de

Klein & Sänger

Waisenhausstrasse 76
80637 Munich (Germany)
T +49 89 15 79 043
F +49 89 15 79 0444
info@ksarc.de
www.ksarc.de

Lussi+Halter Partner AG
dipl. Architekten ETH SIA BSA

Neustadtstrasse 3
6003 Luzern (Switzerland)
T +41 41 226 16 26
F +41 41 226 16 27
info@lussi-halter.ch
www.lussi-halter.ch

kramer biwer mau architekten

Fettstrasse 7a
20357 Hamburg (Germany)
T +49 40 43 27 89 66
F +49 40 43 27 89 68
office@kbm-architekten.de
www.kbm-architekten.de

→24

Dorte Mandrup Arkitekter

Norrebrogade 66D, 1.Sal
2200 Copenhagen (Denmark)
T +45 3393 7350
info@dortemandrup.dk
www.dortemandrup.dk

→210

Marciano Architecture

301 avenue du Prado
13008 Marseille (France)
T +33 4 96 12 09 29
F +33 4 96 12 09 30
agence@remy-marciano.com
www.remy-marciano.com

→188

Daniele Marques, Marques AG

Rankhofstrasse 3
6006 Luzern (Switzerland)
T +41 41 420 19 19
F +41 41 420 60 70
info@marques.ch
www.marques.ch

→58

mattes · sekiguchi partner architekten BDA

Wilhelmstrasse 5a
74072 Heilbronn (Germany)
T +49 7131 20 40 98 0
F +49 7131 20 40 98 9
info@msp-architekten.com
www.msp-architekten.com

→104

Maryann Thompson Architects

14 Hillside Avenue
Cambridge, MA 02140 (USA)
T +1 617 491 41 44
F +1 617 491 38 44
maryann@maryannthompson.com
www.maryannthompson.com

→80, 198

Gordon Murray + Alan Dunlop Architects

Breckenridge House, 274 Sauchiehall Street
Glasgow, G2 3EH (UK)
T +44 141 331 29 26
F +44 141 332 6790
mail@murraydunloparchitects.com
www.murraydunloparchitects.com

→114

no w here architekten

Rotenwaldstrasse 41
70197 Stuttgart (Germany)
T +49 711 6361 831
F +49 711 99 33 145
mail@nowherearchitekten.de
www.nowherearchitekten.de

→62

pbr Planungsbüro Rohling AG

Rheiner Landstrasse 9
49078 Osnabrück (Germany)
T +49 541 94 12 0
F +49 541 94 12 345
info@pbr.de
www.pbr.de

→50

plus+bauplanung GmbH Hübner-Forster-Hübner

Freie Architekten
Goethestrasse 44 / PO 107
72654 Neckartenzlingen (Germany)
T +49 7127 9207 0
F +49 7127 9207 90
info@plus-bauplanung.de
www.plus-bauplanung.de

→184, 240

rheinpark_Architekten

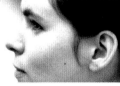

Herner Strasse 137
44809 Bochum (Germany)
T +49 234 41 49 080
F +49 234 41 49 180
post@rheinpark.org
www.rheinpark.org

→118

schulz & schulz

Lamestrasse 6
04107 Leipzig (Germany)
T +49 341 487133
F +49 341 4871345
schulz@schulzarchitekten.de
www.schulzarchitekten.de

→**206**, **260**

SHW Group

5717 Legacy Drive Suite 250
Plano, TX 75024 (USA)
T +1 214 473 2400
F +1 214 473 2401
www.shwgroup.com

→**54**, **142**, **244**

Spaces Architects

B-6 / 109 Basement
Safdarjung Enclave, New Delhi (India)
T +91 011 26161044
F +91 011 26161045
spacesarchitects@rediffmail.com
www.spaces-architects.com

→**66**

Studio Andreas Heller GmbH, Architekten, Designer

Theresienstieg 11
22085 Hamburg (Germany)
T +49 40 471038 0
F +49 40 471038 38
design@studio-andreas-heller.de
www.studio-andreas-heller.de

→**138**

THESKYISBEAUTIFUL

114 Avenue Jean Jaures
Paris (France)
T +84 9 02 12 18 90
tam@theskyisbeautiful.com
www.theskyisbeautiful.com

→**122**

Ramón Pico Valimana + Javier López Rivera ACTA S.L.P.

Calle Imagen 4, 4° D
41003 Sevilla (Spain)
T +34 95 45 64 807
F +34 95 45 62 703
actastudio@gmail.com

→**134**

zanderroth architekten

Karl-Marx-Allee 81
10243 Berlin (Germany)
T +49 30 40 50 57 611
F +49 30 40 50 57 610
kontakt@zanderroth.de
www.zanderroth.de

→**180**

Zyscovivh Architects (Zyscovich, Inc.)

100 N. Biscayne Blvd., 27th Floor
Miami, FL 33132 (USA)
T +1 305 372 5222
F +1 305 577 4521
www.zyscovich.com

→**146**

Imprint

The Deutsche Nationalbibliothek lists this publication in
the Deutsche Nationalbibliografie; detailed bibliographical
data are available on the internet at http://dnb.d-nb.de.

///

ISBN 978-3-03768-023-0

///

© 2010 by Braun Publishing AG
www.braun-publishing.ch

///

///

1st edition 2010

///

Selection of projects: Sibylle Kramer
Project coordination: Marc von Reth
Translation: Cosima Talhouni
Graphic concept: ON Grafik | Tom Wibberenz
Layout: Marc von Reth

///